CONTENTS

INTRODUCTION
· · · · · · · · · · · · · · · · ·

This 15-month guide has been designed and written to give
a concise and accessible insight into both the nature of your
star sign and the year ahead. Divided into two main sections,
the first section of this guide will give you an overview of your
character in order to help you understand how you think,
perceive the world and interact with others and – perhaps just
as importantly – why. You'll soon see that your zodiac sign
is not just affected by a few stars in the sky, but by planets,
elements, and a whole host of other factors, too.

The second section of this guide is made up of daily forecasts.
Use these to increase your awareness of what might appear on
your horizon so that you're better equipped to deal with the
days ahead. While this should never be used to dictate your life,
it can be useful to see how your energies might be affected or
influenced, which in turn can help you prepare for what life
might throw your way.

By the end of these 15 months, these two sections should
have given you a deeper understanding and awareness of
yourself and, in turn, the world around you. There are never
any definite certainties, but with an open mind you will find
guidance for what might be, and learn to take more control of
your own destiny.

THE CHARACTER OF THE LION

....

A Fire sign ruled by the Sun was surely destined to always burn the brightest. Like a moth to a flame, people are naturally drawn to Leonians. Whether singing on a stage, dancing in a club or playing football in the park, they dominate every situation by demanding attention and adoration. Born in the fifth house in the zodiac calendar that represents pleasure and creativity, Leonians often derive immense satisfaction and a sense of purpose from making others happy. These fiery lions can be brimming with confidence or struggle with a lack thereof, and need to be validated with constant praise. The laughter of others is like music to their ears and a career in comedy, like fellow Leonians David Walliams and Jo Brand, could be their calling.

Born in the middle of summer, Leo is a fixed sign that works hard at making dreams become a reality. Daring Leonians Amelia Earhart, Neil Armstrong and Barack Obama achieved historical firsts when realising their dreams. Courageous and not averse to taking risks, fortune definitely favours brave Lions. Second place was not invented for these gold-medal fans. Leonians can be competitive to a fault and should remember that there is more to life than winning. At times, they are exhausting to behold, but fortunately there is plenty to love. What they lack in modesty, Leonians make up for in loyalty and are known for being fiercely committed to loved ones and personal goals. At their best, these charismatic leaders rule with a generous heart and visionary mind.

THE LION

It's hard to miss Leonians when they proudly stride into a room. These beings are the kings and queens of their jungle and expect to be treated as such. Give Leonians the royal treatment and they'll be purring sweetly. However, contradict or disrespect them, and get ready to hear their roar. This sign is fierce but loyal. As true leaders of their pack, Leonians can readily be relied on by their loved ones for giving guidance or doing a favour. Strength and courage are usually the Leonian approach, but they also have a side as soft and beautiful as a Lion's mane. The body part associated with Leo is the heart, and these Lions have big ones. Romance from Leonians will be dramatic and bold. Their lovers should expect to be serenaded in the street or proposed to via a message written in the sky. Go big or go home could be the Leonian mantra, because they were not born to blend into the masses.

THE SUN

The Sun sits at the centre of the universe, and those born under the sign of Leo naturally assume the same position. This makes them charismatic and popular, and, just like the Sun, their absence is felt on days when they are not around. Conversely, there are times when Leonians blaze too forcefully, and those around them must seek shade! However, Leonians can heal just as they can hurt. Apollo is known as one of the Greek gods of the Sun, recognised in part for his ability to heal and protect. Apollo was also associated with music and the arts, a contributing factor perhaps to why this Sun-led sign is drawn to taking centre stage. Whether it's pursuing a creative career in the arts or not, the Sun's influence means Leonians usually have a strong sense of who they are and where they are going in life.

ELEMENTS, MODES AND POLARITIES

Each sign is made up of a unique combination of three defining groups: elements, modes and polarities. Each of these defining parts can manifest themselves in good and bad ways and none should be seen as a positive or a negative – including the polarities! Just like a jigsaw puzzle, piecing these groups together can help illuminate why each sign has certain characteristics and help us find a balance.

ELEMENTS

Fire: Dynamic and adventurous, signs with Fire in them can be extroverted. Others are naturally drawn to them because of the positive light they give off, as well as their high levels of energy and confidence.

Earth: Signs with the Earth element are steady and driven with their ambitions. They make for a solid friend, parent or partner due to their grounded influence and nurturing nature.

Air: The invisible element that influences each of the other elements significantly, Air signs will provide much-needed perspective to others with their fair thinking, verbal skills and key ideas.

Water: Warm in the shallows and freezing as ice. This mysterious element is essential to the growth of everything around it, through its emotional depth and empathy.

MODES

Cardinal: Pioneers of the calendar, cardinal signs jump-start each season and are the energetic go-getters.

Fixed: Marking the middle of the calendar, fixed signs firmly denote and value steadiness and reliability.

Mutable: As the seasons end, the mutable signs adapt and give themselves over gladly to the promise of change.

POLARITIES

Positive: Typically extroverted, positive signs take physical action and embrace outside stimulus in their life.

Negative: Usually introverted, negative signs value emotional development and experiencing life from the inside out.

LEO IN BRIEF

The table below shows the key attributes of Leonians. Use it for quick reference and to understand more about this fascinating sign.

SYMBOL	RULING PLANET	MODE	ELEMENT	HOUSE
♌	☉	⊟	△	♊
The Lion	The Sun	Fixed	Fire	Fifth

COLOUR	BODY PART	POLARITY	GENDER	POLAR SIGN
	🧍	⊕	♂	♒
Purple, Gold	Heart and Spine	Positive	Masculine	Aquarius

ROMANTIC RELATIONSHIPS

. . . .

Leonians are associated with the heart, which is perhaps why they appear to love being in love. They take great pleasure in moving heaven and Earth to romance the socks off their love interests. A Bridget Jones-style kiss in the snow or even standing at the front of a ship like Jack and Rose, these brave Lions will romance their partners as well as any romcom movie character. Whether such bold statements of love appeal is a question of personal taste, yet it's difficult not to fall head over heels for these charismatic charmers.

Leonians are the performers of the calendar and have no problem having all admiring eyes on them. Throw roses at their feet and they will likely provide an encore. Clap too enthusiastically, however, and the Leonian ego may take over. They appreciate partners that shower them with praise, but they should try not to demand it. Practising modesty and channelling a quieter confidence can make Leonians even more charming.

Although the demands of Leonians in love can be great, they will give themselves wholeheartedly to their partners. No expense will be spared in their generous gestures of romance, but it will be their staggering displays of loyalty that will probably be appreciated the most. Once they have set their sights on someone, they will be honest and faithful until the end. Leonians have a fearless approach to love, which can mean that they open themselves up to plenty of heartbreak. Yet their courage is contagious, and their willingness to take risks can lead to the biggest rewards in love.

ARIES: COMPATIBILITY 2/5

Arians are used to being first, but they'll have to learn to share the spotlight and decision-making if they fall for a leader of the jungle. These two signs should recognise clearly their similarities, and therefore know just how to advise and support one another in reaching their goals. With the Leonian led by the heart and the Arian by the head, arguments can be a roaring battlefield when these two don't see eye to eye. Ego and pride will need to be kept in check on both sides if this relationship is to go the distance.

TAURUS: COMPATIBILITY 3/5

Leo is ruled by the Sun and Taurus by Venus; this star and planet are never further away than 48 degrees from each other. The love that these two share is solidified in their sometimes-stubborn commitment to one another. The Lion and Bull are both fixed signs, and this can be their undoing in a long-term relationship when neither one is willing to compromise. Both the Lion and Bull will shower each other with affection and admiration, and will boost each other's self-esteem and be a positive influence in their careers. This couple should just be careful to not let their egos get in the way.

GEMINI: COMPATIBILITY 4/5

The inner Leonian child can be just what the youthful sign of Gemini asked for. This pairing can be like a children's story full of love and adventure, think Peter Pan and Wendy. The high-energy Leonian was born to lead, whilst the mutable Geminian is happy to take this Lion's hand and fly speedily off to Neverland! The Leonian will encourage the Geminian to take an active part in the important choices in their lives. Both positive signs, their extrovert energies and curious natures will see this Air and Fire match embarking on endless adventures.

CANCER: COMPATIBILITY 1/5

Leo is ruled by the Sun and Cancer by the Moon, so this pairing can feel as different as night and day. However, the Lion and the Crab can also find that they have plenty in common to form a lasting love. Born in the fourth and fifth houses that partly signify family and children, the Leonian and Cancerian share a fundamental desire to find that long-term partner to settle down with. Security is essential for the Cancerian and the fixed side of the steadfast Leonian can provide just that. This power couple could go the distance if their differences are embraced.

LEO: COMPATIBILITY 3/5

When a Leonian loves a Leonian, it's like stars colliding and causing a supernova explosion. Beautiful and dramatic, these two creatives are naturally pulled together. With so many Leonians using their talents for the dramatics in the arts, this fiery partnership could readily spark on the set of a movie or from working together in some other creative industry. Actors Ben Affleck and Jennifer Lopez are a prime example. However, like with Affleck and Lopez, a long future together is not always guaranteed. Whilst the fun and romance will be plenty, these two fixed signs may struggle to cooperate.

VIRGO: COMPATIBILITY 2/5

The love of a Leonian can take a Virgoan by surprise; which isn't something the introverted Virgoan is always keen on. The clear differences between the studious Virgoan and show-stopping Leonian can mean that these two might be quick to write each other off as potential partners at first glance. The relationship between this Fire and Earth couple can be a slow burner, but their slow and steady approach could well end up with these two winning the race hand in hand. This couple's strengths are their differences, and these two hard workers can make for a solid and complementary couple.

LIBRA: COMPATIBILITY 4/5

Sitting two places apart on the calendar, a Libran and Leonian can share a compatible partnership. The Libran is an expert in diplomacy, so will likely be able to handle the more dramatic moments in this love affair without bruising the Leonian's ego. Love with the Leonian can be a roller coaster, fun but also consisting of ups and downs. The Libran, symbolised by scales, will hopefully bring a balance to the relationship that the reliable Leonian will appreciate. Ruled by the Sun and Venus, the Leonian and Libran are capable of forming a relationship that is filled with warmth and love.

SCORPIO: COMPATIBILITY 1/5

The love between a watery Scorpian and fiery Leonian can be one of deep intimacy or dampened spirits. Here are two fixed signs that could clash in their different approaches, as they refuse to yield to each other's strong personalities. Shared assets, particularly money, could prove difficult for them. The Scorpian is born in the eighth house where shared possessions are important, and the Leonian belongs in the fourth house where a love of gambling resides. This could result in serious conflict for the couple. If respect is exercised regularly between these two lovers, theirs is a closeness well worth protecting.

SAGITTARIUS: COMPATIBILITY 4/5

This Fire sign match will surely spark with excitement.
Here is a couple in which both partners are likely to plan
a surprise romantic getaway for the other with little or no
notice. Both spontaneous and adventurous, the Leonian and
Sagittarian match each other with their positive energies.
They are probably the dynamic couple that is at the top of
every party invite list. It's not all glittering events, though. The
philosophical Sagittarian and purpose-led Leonian can share a
powerful bond, with an influence that is felt beyond just them.

CAPRICORN: COMPATIBILITY 4/5

A Leonian and Capricornian are the success love story of when
opposites attract. Both tend to have a clear sense of purpose.
For the Leonian, it is in their personal life, and for the
Capricornian it is in their career. Leonian Barack Obama and
Capricornian Michelle Obama are an ideal example of how well
these two can work towards achieving their dreams together.
The Capricornian can show the Leonian what hard work can
accomplish, and the Leonian can bring the fun that sometimes
the cool and dignified Capricornian can be lacking. These are
two very strong characters that can be even stronger together.

AQUARIUS: COMPATIBILITY 5/5

Aquarius is the Air sign that sparks the embers of Leo's Fire element into full blaze. Opposites on the calendar, this combination of shared positive energy, fixed attitudes and complimentary elements makes for two individuals that were astrologically meant to be. These unique characters can be guilty of feeling superior to others, so may need to remind themselves to treat each other as their rightful equals. Foremost, this is a friendship sprung from fun and crafted by a shared creativity. The visionary mind of the Leonian combined with the Aquarian's ideals could have these two creating a utopic life together.

PISCES: COMPATIBILITY 2/5

When a Leonian meets a Piscean, they can bring out the best and worst in each other. The Piscean can be a source of emotional encouragement for the Leonian, whilst the Leonian could help the dreamy Piscean take more action in their life to fully realise dreams. Born in the twelfth house representing sacrifice, the Piscean can be selfless. The Sun-ruled Leonian can be the opposite. When these two sacrificing and self-serving characteristics are felt at their extremes, the relationship can turn toxic. However, the mutable Piscean and fixed Leonian can live in harmony if they both value each other's best qualities.

FAMILY AND FRIENDS

· · · · · · · · · · · · · · · · · ·

All great leaders have a loyal following of subjects, and intrepid Leonians are no exception. Like the Sun, they have the power to draw their friends and families outside so that they can spend time in their warm embrace. Being around heartfelt Lions can lift people's spirits and bring huge amounts of fun and joy. Their outgoing and extroverted energy can be contagious, but it can also be tiring. Fellow positive signs could make for great high-energy friends that can easily keep up with these social butterflies. More introverted negative signs can also play an important role. A friend or family member that Leonians do not constantly have to perform for offer an important change of pace, and an opportunity to recharge.

For all the love and support that Leonians receive from their family and friends, they will give back threefold. They are most known for their unparalleled generosity. Leonians love luxury, so their gifts can be extravagant, whether they have the cash to spoil their loved ones or not. If their bank accounts aren't quite big enough to indulge friends, Leonians can be creative even on the most frugal of budgets. Leonians will share money if they have it but, more importantly, they will always give their valued time and energy to relationships.

Belonging to the fifth house in the calendar that is closely associated with children, the protective and high-spirited Leonian can make a wonderful, and empathetic, parent. In some ways, Leonians never grow up so can remember the frustrations of being young. Their inner children will bring the fun and energy required into raising offspring, or they will be the fun aunt or uncle that their nieces and nephews always want to play with. If Leonians do not have children of their own, other people's will no doubt still gravitate towards them. This makes Leonians the go-to babysitter or first choice of godparent.

Whilst sunny Leonians can have a warm and healing quality, their stage-hogging presence can be overpowering and destructive to their relationships. Their presence and roar is as loud as a Lion's, and it risks drowning out everyone else. It may not be the intention of Leonians to overshadow their friends and family, but the self-led influence from their guiding Sun can turn this confident ruler into a bossy dictator. Their fixed attitudes can make them resistant to the different opinions of others, but Leonians should be careful of surrounding themselves with only yes-men. A diverse social network where everyone has a voice is the only kingdom worthy of Leonian leadership.

MONEY AND CAREERS

· · · · · · · · · · · · · · · · ·

Being a particular star sign will not dictate that you follow a certain type of career, but it can help you to identify potential areas for thriving in. Conversely, to succeed in the workplace, it is just as important to understand strengths and weaknesses to achieve career and financial goals.

A love for luxury and aristocratic tendencies creates a risk for Leonians to become too focused on the material things in life. It can be good to enjoy a little luxury in life, as long as they don't let it dominate everything they do. However, if they can channel their love for grand things creatively, they could follow in the footsteps of notable Leonian fashion designers such as Yves Saint-Laurent, Coco Chanel and Michael Kors. Rather than wearing the designer names of others, Leonians possess a passion for luxury and leadership that could help them become the next big name that everyone is coveting.

Whilst Leonians enjoy the best in life, they will generally be sensible with their finances and not spend beyond their means. A trip to Vegas might be tempting, but they aren't usually the type to go for broke and risk losing it all. The fixed part of Leonians will keep their spending steady, unwilling to risk losing their financial security. They may be driven to earn lots of money so that they can buy all the luxuries they desire, but they will probably earn their fortune through organised efforts and a steadfast approach rather than at the slot machines.

Whether Leonians go for the leading roles in a film or strive after leading a country, they will be comfortable in the spotlight of their choice. Leonians' natural self-assurance makes them authoritative and confident figures, and others will respect that, if given the opportunity. So whether it's the moves of Leonian Mick Jagger, the skills of Harry Kane or the leadership of Barack Obama, all eyes will be firmly on them.

If fame doesn't appeal, managerial roles could be a natural domain in many industries, be it on a football field or in an office. Occupations in the world of luxury are also appealing, given Leonians' appreciation of the finer things in life. But no matter the field, being boss is often the primary goal, although a bossy attitude should to be avoided wherever possible to keep others happy.

As with family, colleagues cannot be chosen. Therefore, it can be advantageous to use star signs to learn about their key characteristics and discover the best ways of working together. Part of the attraction for becoming a leader for Leonians is the competition. The king or queen of the jungle loves to demonstrate their prowess and rise above any competitors. However, Leonians can be dominating and may need to remind themselves that there is no 'I' in 'team', especially if they are working with other 'me first' characters, such as Arians. Taureans might share the same ambitious dreams as Leonians, but any colleague that is also fixed will need to work harder at compromise.

HEALTH AND WELLBEING

· · · · · · · · · · · · · · · · · ·

These bold Lions can also be highly sensitive souls. Like anyone, they have their ups and downs, so friends and family can be essential supporters that straighten the crown on their ruler's head. The critical words of Virgoans might be felt too harshly by sensitive Leonians, and knock their confidence further if they are already feeling low. Pisceans or Cancerians could tread more carefully, and be the emotionally encouraging friends that help Leonians stride forwards again. A need for constant reassurance can stem from a crisis in confidence, so Leonians should work on building up their own self-esteem from within so that they do not have to always rely on others to lift them out of their low moods. Owning their mistakes and recognising where they can improve are just a couple of ways that Leonians can grow to become happier and humble.

Winning can feel wonderful, but when Leonians reach their desired peak, they may find themselves at a loss. Once Leonians rise to the top of their profession, they may need to take up another hobby or avenue of interest to satisfy their urge to win. Throwing themselves into a competitive sport that takes them outside will appease their ambitious side, youthful energy and love of the Sun. Whilst protection from harmful UV rays is important, spending time in the Sun sensibly can be just as vital for keeping healthy. Apart from receiving essential Vitamin D, sunshine's healing properties also extend to lowering cholesterol and reducing high blood pressure – wonderful news for heart-associated Leonians. Learning lines for their latest play in the sunshine, or swimming in a lido rather than an indoor swimming pool, could also help improve physical and mental health.

Guided by the Sun, representing the self and life purpose, Leonians seem to know who they are and where they are going. At least that's what it can look like from the standpoint of admiring onlookers. If Leonians lack direction in life, it can be a major source of upset for them. They may feel they are not living up to their own expectations or the expectations of others. Leonians should try to take the pressure off themselves, and understand that learning who they truly are and where they wish to get to in life are two big questions that plague everyone. They would do well to cut themselves some slack, and not get bogged down by their reputation of always being the best. The high status of the charismatic, larger than life Lion can be a burden to Leonians that feel they don't fit the bill. They are essentially best at being themselves, whatever form that may take, so should not attempt to cage themselves within the confines of expectation.

Leo

....

DAILY FORECASTS
for 2020

OCTOBER

Thursday 1st
October starts with a Full Moon in your travel sector. What is being highlighted now are seeds you may have planted back in March. Any plans you have made to see other cultures and explore new lands are now open for question. You have been given the green light, so make the most of the opportunity.

Friday 2nd
Venus has now entered a great part of your chart. She is sat in your sector that deals with money, beauty, harmony and value, bringing you much good fortune. She will be there for the whole of the month, so be sure to make the most of October and the blessings it brings with it.

Saturday 3rd
You have a lovely aspect shining on you from above. Venus is in harmony with the Moon, so your wants and needs are balanced between this planetary pair. The Moon is also accentuating your need for beauty, allowing you to assess what it is that you value the most. Take a moment to appreciate it.

Sunday 4th
You may feel conflicted today. After revelling in the recent easy days, you now have a moment of anxiety. Your mind is making up excuses not to value material things and wants you to find worth in deep, spiritual activities. These are not mutually exclusive values - you can do both.

Monday 5th

Pluto, the lord of power and control, joins the other big planets in your health and duty sector and goes direct. You will begin to feel more control over your daily routine, and any health issues may get some reprieve now. You feel more satisfaction in the nine to five, take the time to be productive and get ahead!

Tuesday 6th

A great day for socialising, get out there and entertain your friends. Everyone knows you can put on a show or great dinner, so be that person today. Hosting a get-together or attending one will give you equal pleasure. Find fulfilment in company with good friends, good food and good times.

Wednesday 7th

Be careful what you say today. Mercury is opposing Uranus, the planet of shocks and surprises, and that could lead to trouble in your family or career. Just be mindful to think before you speak, otherwise you could hurt someone close to you. Alternatively, it could be you on the receiving end, but try not to hold on to any unintended insults.

Thursday 8th

Today is one of those days where retreat, solitude or simply being quiet is recommended. Enjoy the comfort foods you liked as a child and watch a good box set, your favourite film, or curl up with a fantastic book. Switch off and enjoy a little fantasy. Have a comfortable day in your pyjamas and soothe your soul.

Friday 9th

You are still enjoying some downtime and eating ice cream straight from the tub, yet you also have the desire to make a change. Keep it simple, such as rearranging your living space or clearing some clutter. Mars, who helps us move, is at odds with Pluto, so overhauling anything that is complicated could prove difficult. Think before you act.

Saturday 10th

All systems have been recharged and you are feeling motivated again. Your emotional needs are not entirely synchronised with your commitments, but you can still sail through the day easily. Some pleasant surprises or unexpected gifts could come your way. Enjoy the small things, and don't fret about the big ones.

Sunday 11th

Oh dear, you are back to a day where things may not go so well. The Moon is in your sign, but it is also making some bad connections to Uranus and Mercury. It is another day where you will need to curb the urge to say something potentially outrageous or hurtful. You can't take things back once said, so take a moment before you speak.

Monday 12th

A day of contemplation today. You will be looking back at where you have been, as well as forwards to where you would like to go. What skills can you take into the future, and what definitely needs to be left behind? Do nothing except consider this, it isn't time for action yet but time for consolidating your past and future.

Tuesday 13th

Tempers could flare today. There is heightened tension because the Sun is shining right on Mars in your travel sector. Mars is still retrograde and not getting where he wants to go, so the best plan is to try and see what his lesson is. Take a breath if the pressure gets too much, don't act out of anger.

Wednesday 14th

Mercury retrograde warning! A big part of yesterday's tension was a preview for the next couple of weeks. Mercury has been thinking about, talking about and listening to everyone's secrets and he may just be ready to reveal all. Keep your counsel until it is all over. Some things are not yours to tell, and you don't want to cross boundaries.

Thursday 15th

You could find yourself involved in a power struggle today. You do what is expected of you, but someone may push for more. Stand your ground. You give enough of yourself to certain people and that is commendable. Any more would be exhausting. Saying 'no' is an important part of taking care of yourself sometimes.

Friday 16th

A New Moon in your area of short journeys and communication is a chance to make mini resolutions and plant seeds for new projects and new paths. This one is in Libra and asks you to consider where you end and another begins. Aim for harmony and balance in how you speak to others and honour their boundaries.

Saturday 17th

Your family sector is in the spotlight today. Saying what is on your mind and in your heart feels imperative. This could be upsetting, but it's necessary for growth. Emotions can run deep now, and kind, supportive words are needed. You can tell the truth without being hurtful and being gentle can help make difficult topics easier to handle.

Sunday 18th

How can you find a happy medium between duty and leisure time? Today feels like an 'all work and no play' day. How can you best serve your community and help others, without wearing yourself down too much? Health can become a concern if you feel that you give more of yourself than you should. Remember to rest.

Monday 19th

Jupiter is getting attention from both Venus and Mars today. Jupiter and Venus get along well and he helps her to develop anything that you value, such as money or belongings. Mars, on the other hand, is not happy with Jupiter, and is unable to move on with his exploration. This may mean you feel conflicted, but it will pass.

Tuesday 20th

Remember that Mercury is still retrograde. Today he is opposite Uranus, who will be occupying your career sector for some years to come. Be careful not to upset your boss. Vent with close friends if you need to complain about work and keep your game face on professionally. Don't make a mistake which could have long term impacts.

Wednesday 21st

You may still be unstable in the workplace today, and there could be power struggles. However, with Venus in your area of love and money, you may be able to sweet-talk your boss into thinking you are due a rise. Who dares wins, but be sure to tread softly so you don't ruffle any feathers.

Thursday 22nd

The Sun enters Scorpio today, which means you are likely to investigate intense emotions within your family of origin. Mother issues could surface now. Be careful of aggression and watch out for small accidents. When in doubt, don't rush into any thoughtless speech or make any rash decisions. When emotions run high it's always better to take stock before you act.

Friday 23rd

Wear your heart on your sleeve and spend quality time with a loved one today. The Moon and Venus are in a good connection to make the next couple of days sweet and romantic. If you are single, take some time to be nice to your shadow and treat yourself to something special. Pamper yourself thoroughly.

Saturday 24th

You have a knack of getting what you want today, so ask for it. Spending time with someone special can be especially enjoyable if you can arrange it. You will have a harmonious day ruled over by Venus, who is sweet-talking Saturn into relaxing the rules a little. Have fun letting your hair down a little, there's no pressure today.

Sunday 25th

Mercury is lost in the glare of the Sun, so you may find that you have nothing to say today and prefer to remain silent. The Moon moves into your sex, death and transformation sector, so sit back and watch the show. You may learn more from observing your own emotions and those around you, and this could be valuable for the future.

Monday 26th

An easy flow of surreal energy is suddenly surrounding you, and it feels wonderful. You could be floating on cloud nine or away with the fairies. Getting high on life is prescribed for you, so make the most of this dreamy day. It's nice to indulge your whimsical side from time to time, and this might result in a burst of creativity.

Tuesday 27th

You continue to have that feel-good factor around you and it is quite intoxicating. You and your significant other are addicted to each other today too. Enjoy the ride and make sure you come back down to earth gently. If you are single, you will feel like a million dollars. Celebrate everything that makes you amazing.

Wednesday 28th

Mercury is reversing into your communication sector. Although he likes being there, the reason for his visit is to ask you how you make yourself heard in friendship circles. Are you pushy or placid? At the same time, Venus also enters this area and will address the fairness of these friendships. You may be able to find balance through their intervention.

Thursday 29th

Today you will feel very passionate about a new project you have had in mind. You will want to get it off the ground but retrograde Mars is not in a position to add his energy to it. You will have to wait a while, so put it on the back burner. Take the time to finesse it and get it really ready.

Friday 30th

Here comes another day where your career is taking up more space in your head than anything else. There is nothing wrong with this. You might be putting your heart and soul into a work project and want to be recognised for it. Quite rightly so. Don't shy away from making sure you get the credit you're due, but try not to step on toes or brag.

Saturday 31st

A Blue Moon, the second Full Moon in a calendar month, occurs in your career sector today. This might reveal some startling facts about the workplace. Keep your eyes and ears open, and you may well learn something to your advantage. Remember that discretion can be the better part of valour however, use your judgement in how you utilise this information.

NOVEMBER

. . . .

Sunday 1st

The Moon in your career sector gets a helping hand from
Jupiter in your daily routine sector. Work stress could get
bigger, but in a way that will ultimately benefit you by bringing
potential opportunities. There may be some disturbances
at work or some exciting new developments. Keep yourself
informed and be ready for anything.

Monday 2nd

Even though it is just the start of the week, you feel the need
to be out and about with friends. Social networking or post-
work drinks could be just the things to ease you in gently.
Saturn in your daily routine sector gives you the go-ahead.
Enjoy yourself, but remember that some boundaries should be
respected with colleagues which aren't there with friends.

Tuesday 3rd

The Moon acts as an anchor and holds Mars and Venus
together, so it is a good time for dealing with the opposite
sex and settling arguments. Travel and communication are
highlighted for you today. Do you have a long-distance love
interest? Could this be a possibility now? Use this opportunity
for open discussion to build bridges and broach new ideas.

Wednesday 4th

Mercury goes direct in your short journeys and communications sector. It is time to apologise sincerely for things that may have caused hurt. You can also now think about travel without any disruptions or cancellations. You feel a sense of moving towards your future and where you are meant to be. This is excellent progress, but don't try to rush.

Thursday 5th

It is a dreamy kind of day, where you make plans in your head and build castles in the sky. Feeling adrift from everyone else, you want to stay in your comfort zone physically but retreat into the fantasy world in your mind. Indulge yourself if you are able, or plan something for a later date that you can look forward to.

Friday 6th

You are still feeling the need to be wrapped in cotton wool, but you have a sense of guilt about doing so. Your rational mind kicks in and tries to pull you out if it. Stay there a little longer if you can, and you will be ready for action when you reappear. Don't be rushed out of your comfort zone.

Saturday 7th

The Moon moves into your sign today. How will you use this energy? You are feeling needy and may be stroppy or throw tantrums if those needs are not met. You can't always get what you want, so focus on what you need instead. Don't throw your toys out of the pram if your wishes aren't immediately fulfilled.

Sunday 8th

Static energy will leave you pacing up and down your room wanting to roar but unable to. You feel frustrated. This will soon pass, so try to focus on one thing and see it through to the end. A sense of accomplishment is what you need now. Are there any projects you have in progress or need to do which can give you a quick win?

Monday 9th

This could be another testing day. Venus and Mars are in direct opposition and there will be a clash between the sexes or around issues regarding travel. This will be irritating and may see you spending too much money on pretty things that you don't need. Put the wallet away. There are other ways to smooth ruffled feathers.

Tuesday 10th

There is an intense urge for balance right now. A 'now or never' feel hangs over the day. You want to get something out of your mouth before the right moment passes. This could involve you taking a short trip to do so, rather than by emailing or texting, as some things are better when said face to face.

Wednesday 11th

Being thorough is what is needed today. Pay attention to what money is coming in and what is going out. You will be thinking about how much you spend on yourself, as well as how much time and money goes out to others. Is the money going towards valuable things which give you genuine joy? If not, stop spending.

Thursday 12th

As the Moon moves into your short journeys and communications sector, she bumps into Venus and they talk about love, beauty and harmony. At the same time, Jupiter and Pluto are sitting together wondering what they can change in your work and service sector. They want to make something bigger and better. This could be a great opportunity, but don't get too carried away.

Friday 13th

A mystery-solving Moon moves into your family sector and makes a connection to the Jupiter and Pluto tactic talks. You may find that this is about how you devote yourself to others, especially family. How might you transform existing duties and make them more worthwhile? How can you make sure your family time is high quality?

Saturday 14th

You will feel the sense of pressure lift as Mars goes direct in your travel sector. He wants to move forwards, but this has been a frustrating time in this area for you both. Things will pick up again and you will realise that you were stuck for a very good reason. Take your time to unpick problems and see how they can be avoided in future.

Sunday 15th

A New Moon in your family sector gives you the opportunity to start afresh with issues pertaining to mother, ancestry and family. As this all takes place in Scorpio, the new starts could be something that go deep and far back. You could find some gold in your family history, if you take the time to look.

Monday 16th

Power and control issues are likely today, as Venus is confronted by Pluto, who craves control. Venus will probably win, and for you that means that these issues could be about sibling rivalry. Keep your roar to yourself, and don't try to start a fight where there isn't one. Things will settle down again shortly.

Tuesday 17th

Mercury has been diving deep into your family sector but today he is opposite Uranus, so prepare for a shocking revelation. Your mood will turn to the past and thoughts of where you have been to get where you are now will surface. Take lessons from this and see how you can use them to move forwards.

Wednesday 18th

Feeling stuck in a rut? Your need for action, adventure and exploration is being hampered by a pull from the Moon in your duties sector. What is holding you back from the pioneering lifestyle that is attracting you now? This mood will pass quickly, so just stay with your thoughts instead of chasing a passing fancy.

Thursday 19th

Emotionally, you may feel pulled in different directions today. This is a good opportunity to check in with your health and look at where your energy is going. There is a lesson to be learnt about who and what drains you to the point of exhaustion. Are these necessary in your life? If they are, how can you best recharge?

Friday 20th

Relationships, especially with significant others, are highlighted today. It is not an easy energy as the Moon is making uncomfortable aspects to Uranus and Mercury. Both of these planets can be unpredictable, and you or someone close could say or do something regrettable. Best to lie low, take it easy and wait for it to blow over.

Saturday 21st

The Sun moves into your creative sector so it is time to play. You will feel more enthusiastic about getting out, making, playing, laughing and putting yourself on show. This is a favourable month for Fire signs like you so enjoy yourself and make the most of it. Venus brings harmony to your family sector too.

Sunday 22nd

You require depth in conversations today. Triviality just will not do. Partnerships can be explored and enriched with discussions about secrets and anything taboo. Sex, death and rebirth fascinate you, and you are eager to learn more about what makes another person tick. Have fun with it but remember to respect boundaries, as not everyone may be as comfortable as you are.

Monday 23rd

You may still be exploring mystical subjects today and, as the Moon joins Neptune, may be tempted to disappear off into an imaginary land. Choose a fantasy film or novel to get lost in and write down any inspiring ideas you may find there. Allow your creativity to run free, you can reap the rewards later.

Tuesday 24th

You now want to get out and conquer new lands, explore new frontiers. Other cultures will appeal, as will other religions. You have many plans in your head and feel upbeat and positive. Making a vision board or ticking off countries on a map could be a nice activity if you can't get away for real. Plan for a new trip and remember previous ones.

Wednesday 25th

Mercury is in your family sector, and is talking to Neptune in your sex, death and rebirth sector. Together, they are gathering information on family backgrounds. Secrets and lies can surface now. Intrigue is possible, but as it is in the past it is best left there instead of stirring up old hurts. No finger pointing required.

Thursday 26th

Your get up and go has got up and gone today. Your emotional energy does not match your physical energy and you will feel drained. You have needs to fill but you are held back by your daily routine and possibly health worries. You need an energy boost in a gentle way. Try a good belly laugh.

Friday 27th

Today we have Venus opposite Uranus, which is basically a fight between harmony and disruption. This occurs in your family and career sectors. These sectors can also be about the legacy you will leave, as well as the one you have inherited. Watch out for a financial matter that's about to erupt too. Try to steer straight and ride out the storm.

Saturday 28th

Things can seem a bit surreal for you now. There may be some aftershocks that knock you off balance. Try to get grounded by eating, taking a walk or chatting to a trusted friend. Doing physical exercise will help too, centring yourself in your body and giving you an endorphin boost. Just remember to breathe.

Sunday 29th

You will want to get out and be sociable now. You need friends around at this time, if just to maintain some sense of normality. Being the centre of attention is not what you need, so try letting someone else have a turn. Giving someone else the reins will give you the break you need and could lead to wonderful things.

Monday 30th

A Full Moon and partial eclipse in your social sector may make things a little unpredictable. This is actually a good thing, so go along with it and see where it leads. You may find something new and exciting is staring you in the face just waiting for you to say yes. Be brave and make a change.

DECEMBER

· · · · · · · · · · · · · · · · · ·

Tuesday 1st

You will begin December by listening to your heart and its
yearnings. Feeling creative and playful comes naturally to you,
but there is an added sense of adventure too, particularly at
this time of year. You will wonder about the big, wide world
and what exactly is out there for you to discover.

Wednesday 2nd

You will have another one of those days where you just want
to be left alone and wallow in your dreams. Switching off
and taking a break will be good for you. Shut your door, pull
up the duvet and read a good book or watch a film. Self-care
sometimes means taking time off and being still.

Thursday 3rd

Why is it that you will not allow yourself some free time? Yes,
yours is a fire sign, but even a fire knows how to burn quietly.
Action is not favoured today as your heart is not in it, but you
have a habit of making yourself feel guilty for standing still.
Slow down a little.

Friday 4th

The Moon moves into your sign today, helping you get your
fire back. Mercury is in your creative sector and is whispering
in your ear about projects he would like to see you do. He will
start shouting loudly if you do not pay attention, but don't let
him bully you into making changes you aren't ready for.

Saturday 5th

The Moon and Mars, both in Fire signs, give you the motivation you need to get on with things today. The only thing to watch out for is the Moon's uneasy connection to Uranus in your career sector. Be wary of possible unrest at work, keep your head down and get on with your own tasks.

Sunday 6th

A positive flow of energy between Venus and Neptune brings harmony to your sex, death and rebirth sector. Shared finances also feature today and, as Venus loves money, this can only be a good thing. Just be careful that this is not one of Neptune's illusions. Wait before making any big decisions, check they're right for you.

Monday 7th

Money is on your mind again today, as the Moon moves into this sector. Some nice surprises may come your way in the form of gifts or innovative ideas, perfect for the holiday season. Work with this energy and allow yourself to feel pleased about whatever this brings. You deserve it.

Tuesday 8th

Everything is ticking along nicely at the moment. Time management comes easily and you can fit in work, play and helping others. Being good to yourself by scheduling in a gym session or relaxing massage will really benefit your health. Try and keep this balance up in the coming days, you will be glad of the wellbeing it brings.

Wednesday 9th

Catching up with friends and family via text message, social media or email will be the theme for today. You can bring harmony and balance within relationships, if you so choose. You have an easy-going manner and people will be drawn to your magnetic charm. You enjoy being needed, but don't give too much of yourself or you will become exhausted.

Thursday 10th

Venus helps you to relax some control issues that may have been going on in your family sector. This is likely to be where family members have been demanding your time and presence, but it is important that you establish boundaries for yourself. Try not to hold on to anything that is a myth or an illusion.

Friday 11th

Emotional shocks are likely now in your family sector. Uncomfortable issues from the past come back to be healed. This is not your job, but if you use compassion you can be a great leader in this. If you are not directly involved, show integrity by keeping out of it. There is nothing to be gained from interfering.

Saturday 12th

The two female energies of the Moon and Venus sit closely together in your family sector. Listen to female voices in particular today. Mothers, grandmothers, aunts and sisters will have the knowledge and wisdom that you need to hear, even if it's not something you want to hear. Organise a powwow and listen up.

Sunday 13th

The Moon enters your creative sector and self-expression comes easily now. You can be centre stage, but do so with the leadership qualities that you possess. Being narcissistic and demanding is not going to get you anywhere, instead concentrate on building up your team to aim for the stars together. Laugh, sing and play. Shine in your glory.

Monday 14th

A New Moon in your creative sector can see you beginning an art project or endeavour that you put your heart and soul into. Venus and Jupiter are in a good connection, and will help this new project to be beautiful and grow in the way you wish. Nurturing this will bring you pleasure and nurture your soul at the same time.

Tuesday 15th

Venus steps into your creative sector so anything that you begin now has her blessing. This could be love, money or beautifying your home. The energy and motivation you need will be provided by Mars, while the ideas will come courtesy of Mercury. This planetary dream team will help you maximise your creative flair and get things done.

Wednesday 16th

You could be decluttering today and making space in your life for new things to come in. There is a chance to follow your dreams and manifest something you have been longing to do for a while. Creating a vision board may help you to focus, and see what needs to be removed before starting a new quest.

Thursday 17th

The Moon is busy today with Jupiter and Saturn. Jupiter, on the last degree of your daily routine sector, is urging you to think big before moving onwards. Saturn is making sure you have done all the research before moving into your relationship sector. This is a big time for you. Listen to both planets, be fearless but make sure you have prepared.

Friday 18th

Mercury, who is in your creative sector, is dazzled by the Sun today. You may experience a little brain fog, so use this opportunity to think with your heart instead. On the other hand, you may be overloaded with bright ideas and will want to write them all down. These notes can help you see what you're thinking without mental noise.

Saturday 19th

Your inner world and outer appearance are in synch today, and you are able to express what is in your heart. Inner peace wraps you comfortably, and there is a glow around you that attracts people. Work with this. Meditation or yoga can help extend the feelings and will be extra effective with your current balance.

Sunday 20th

This is a big day in the heavens. Jupiter and Saturn are on the same degree in your love and relationship sector. This may be experienced as a 'push and pull' type of energy, so you might feel torn between two alternatives. Listen carefully and you might hear the lessons that they are trying to teach you.

Monday 21st

Today, the Sun and Mercury move into your daily duties sector. The next few weeks will be a chance to take a good look at your routine and give your health an overhaul, bringing a new you in the new year. The Winter Solstice occurs in this sector too, so enjoy the darkness of the longest night.

Tuesday 22nd

You may be feeling on edge, with over-indulgent seasonal treats and parties all around. You have a restless heart, coupled with an urge to get out and about, which may be hampered by the dark winter weather. You need new initiatives to explore or fresh projects to start. Sit tight. The restlessness will pass and then you can move forwards.

Wednesday 23rd

You may feel some anger rising and will want to throw things out the window, including any recent ideas you may have had. This is due to uneasy connections between the Moon (emotions), Mars (motion) and Pluto (control). Manage the small things today and leave the bigger ones for tomorrow. Endeavour not to let your negative emotions get the better of you.

Thursday 24th

You are eager to start building something. Could this be your empire? You've had many new ideas seeding this year and now feel they can be planted. Your career needs to be reviewed or last-minute jobs completed before the holidays. Try to get work finished so that you can enjoy the time with your loved ones without distraction.

Friday 25th

Merry Christmas! Despite the holiday today, you feel restless
and would rather just get on with your new plans while you
have momentum. There is a lot of chatter going on about work
and the mundane jobs you do, sometimes for others. Leave
the angst and enjoy your family's company. Fathers and sons
feature greatly.

Saturday 26th

You can resume dreaming up your big vision. You have this
under control, and know exactly what you want and how you
are going to get it. This is something you are not going to let
anyone else take over, and you love having full control over your
project, setting your own agenda. Dream big, you deserve it.

Sunday 27th

Today, you can spend time with friends and tell them your new
plans. You will be seen as innovative and unusual, and friends
will want to join your happiness party. Be aware that you, and
you alone, need to steer this ship, but that there is nothing
wrong with gathering allies and sound advice. Outside input
can always provide valuable perspective.

Monday 28th

You will have a series of 'light-bulb moments' today. Ideas are
coming thick and fast, and you can see the road ahead far into
the future. This may only be in your dreams, but stick with it
and don't get discouraged if things seem out of reach right now.
Your determination is the factor that will propel you forwards.

Tuesday 29th

A Full Moon in your dreaming sector asks you to look back at the last six months. What have you managed to manifest without realising it? This may also be to do with family and especially mothers. A reward may be offered today or you could give yourself a well-deserved pat on the back.

Wednesday 30th

You may want to keep your thoughts to yourself today, staying out of any trouble which might appear. Take some 'me time' and lie low. Venus in your creative sector is not very happy with Neptune in your sex, death and rebirth sector. She is seeing money spent on trivial items and does not approve.

Thursday 31st

Congratulations for getting through 2020. Planetary alignments were tough this year, but you did well and made it to 2021. Any celebrating you do tonight can have a Scorpian theme to it. Secrets and lies may surface, which could be erotic and sexy. Have a good evening and stay safe. Some risks can be fun, but don't be too reckless.

Leo

DAILY FORECASTS
for 2021

JANUARY

· · · · · · · · · · · · · · · · · ·

Friday 1st

Happy New Year and welcome to 2021. You begin the year
with the Moon in your sign. After a Full Moon in your hidden
sector, you may feel that all eyes are on you. Show yourself in
your very best aspect now. Be brave, outgoing and the star of
your own show.

Saturday 2nd

Mars, the warrior planet is on the last part of your travel
sector. Make the most of this energy by planning future
trips or higher education courses. Mars in his home sign is
powerful, he will help you make good resolutions for the year
and they will probably stick.

Sunday 3rd

Today you ensure that everything is in order. Perhaps you
decide to do some decluttering. New planners and diaries will
excite you. Your career is on your mind and you may have
some bold new ideas to discuss back at work. Be super-efficient
now and impress someone in the workplace.

Monday 4th

The Moon sits opposite Neptune today. This outer planet is
connected to your dreams and illusions, you may discover
something is not tangible enough for you to grasp. Neptune
in your intimacy sector is also concerned with finances.
Check money you may have invested and look at your
personal finances.

Tuesday 5th

The influence coming from Mercury and Pluto meeting in your health and duties sector suggests that you have a need to control how your time and energy are used. There may be a lot of short trips or communication requiring you to be of service to others today.

Wednesday 6th

Mars is about to leave your travel sector. It's critical that you know just what your plans for the year are. If you make a long list, realise that you may not fulfil all of them. Put that Martian energy into the ones that are worth your sustained effort.

Thursday 7th

The Moon urges you to assess anything you see or hear before you respond. Pluto is at odds with the Moon and can make you feel manipulated. Use your observation skills and weigh up a situation today. Self-control will help you not get drawn into other people's dramas.

Friday 8th

This morning you will feel torn between following your head or your heart. Mercury the messenger planet may be telling you things which are simply malicious gossip. Alternatively, he may be urging you to change something now. When the Moon shifts this afternoon, you get more clarity.

Saturday 9th

A deep and intense Moon makes you yearn for security.
The best place to be is at home. Venus moves into your
health and duties sector, making sure that you are taking
good care of yourself. Mercury flies into your relationship
sector, watch communication between yourself and partner
come alive.

Sunday 10th

Romantic conversations are encouraged by a good connection
between Venus and Mars. Mercury sits with Saturn and has a
good talk about how to respect other's boundaries and protect
your own. This is an important lesson from Saturn who will
dominate your relationship sector for two and a half years.

Monday 11th

Mercury visits with Jupiter, also in your relationship sector.
Jupiter brings joy, expansion and spiritual growth. Perhaps
you have found someone with whom you can have great
conversations. Making plans to rebel or change the world
together will be an excellent adventure for you this year.
Make it happen.

Tuesday 12th

Be brave and express bold, new ideas in the workplace. What
have you got to lose? You might rock a boat or two but there
is sense in your words. You are outspoken but not pushy. It's
possible that you may have picked someone's sore spots.

Wednesday 13th

A New Moon in your health and duties sector is another chance to set those New Year resolutions in stone. This Moon has endurance and responsibility packed into it. Mars and Saturn are also in the mix making you a powerhouse in your work and personal relationships. Be direct but be kind.

Thursday 14th

The Sun meets Pluto today. This is highly charged ego stuff. In the heat of the Sun, your ruler, something is transformed and forever changed. You can make gold from lead today if you desire. Burn off what no longer serves you. Relationships are blessed today.

Friday 15th

Today you get a chance to breathe. You may find that you are standing amongst wreckage that needs clearing. Know that this is a good thing, you can travel onwards with a lighter load. Do not look back or even think about searching through the garbage. Leave it well alone.

Saturday 16th

You may be feeling emotionally drained and in need of downtime. Merging with your very closest tribe or simply being alone will help. The Moon in your intimacy sector helps you to switch off and process your thoughts. Spiritual connections and a yearning to know deeper mysteries fill your mind.

Sunday 17th

As the Moon meets Neptune, anything you think you may have grasped slips away from you. This monthly connection can add to a feeling of disconnect. Sometimes this can be a good thing. Be careful not to self-medicate with unhealthy coping mechanisms. Use this time to process deep concepts.

Monday 18th

Jupiter and Uranus are not friendly today. This can mean there is disruption in your partnerships. Uranus in your career sector is causing a rumbling and the connection to Jupiter is making it bigger than necessary. You may have a tantrum and this will affect your business and personal relationships.

Tuesday 19th

The Sun moves into your relationship sector now. You will discover that there is extra warmth and joy to go around all your acquaintants. Sharing the love or rebelling against offers made to you will be the theme for the next month. Words of love can soothe you today.

Wednesday 20th

Mars and Uranus meet in your career sector. This is a highly volatile connection as Mars the Warrior and Uranus the disruptor will stir up trouble. However, this energy can be used to good effect. Brainstorming, networking and being productive are favoured under this explosive influence. Use it wisely.

Thursday 21st

The Moon now joins Mars and Neptune. You will be emotionally challenged to behave correctly. Perhaps you don't feel good enough at work and this unsettles you. Concern yourself with being slow, steady and focused. Let all the dramas happen and do not get drawn into them.

Friday 22nd

Today you may find that communications are not easy. Mercury is chatting away in your relationship sector and distracting you. Venus and Pluto help to make loving changes and keep your mind on the job in hand. Just do what you need to do and nothing more for now.

Saturday 23rd

The Moon slips into your social sector in time for the weekend. This is a good time to be with your tribe and brainstorm ideas. You might also benefit from letting off steam or analysing recent events with friends. Venus and Neptune allow you to let go and relax.

Sunday 24th

Today you think about what the future holds and how you can make that happen. Jupiter links in and expands your world view. You're yearning for culture, education and travel. Your ruler, the mighty Sun, sits with Saturn and illuminates your responsibilities. You may feel restricted or proud.

Monday 25th

Mars and Jupiter square off. You have the necessary discipline in your career sector but lack the motivation right now. This may be getting you down. You feel this intensely today as Jupiter is expanding any feeling Mars is influencing. Today, it is your lack of self-worth.

Tuesday 26th

The Moon moves into your hidden sector. You can be quite intuitive now and know what's best for you. Favourite foods or binge watching a good TV show will make you feel better. Mothers or female relatives can be a great source of comfort to you. Nurture yourself.

Wednesday 27th

The Moon is now sitting opposite Venus and Pluto. You may feel manipulated or used. It is up to you how much you do for other people, don't climb a mountain for those who wouldn't return the favour. Stay in your nest until this feeling passes.

Thursday 28th

A Full Moon in your sign helps you stand up and roar. However, other planetary connections make this Moon unstable. It's likely that your strength has returned, and you become pushy, obnoxious and self-righteous today. This isn't a good look, try being someone others would follow and not a tyrant.

Friday 29th

The Sun and Jupiter meet up. If you were a spoilt brat yesterday, then today you will be worse. Egos may clash badly. If you have played nicely, then this connection brings a blessing. Relationships are highly favoured under this lucky influence. Love will shine all around.

Saturday 30th

With a Mercury retrograde starting tomorrow, use today to prepare. Back up all your devices, double-check travel plans and be mindful with communications. This retrograde occurs in your relationship sector. You will need to tread carefully and ensure that no-one misunderstands your words. You may become quite rebellious.

Sunday 31st

Check your bank balance and spend time with your 'to do' list today. Make sure that you have left nothing incomplete as Mercury retrograde will seek this out. Try not to get distracted by the call from Neptune to switch off, there is work to be done.

FEBRUARY

....

Monday 1st

Venus floats into your relationship sector where she will do her best to harmonise the effects of Mercury's retrograde. This is good news as there's tension forming between your career and relationships. Have you been over-working and neglecting a loved one? You're strict on yourself today for no reason.

Tuesday 2nd

You're often the mediator when it comes to communication. You have the ability to see things from all angles and rarely judge without scrutiny. Today you may be called upon for these skills. You may have to do something for the greater good and justify it later.

Wednesday 3rd

Venus and Mars are not talking today. This can bring troubles in your sectors of relationships and career. Try to keep them separate. This afternoon you take a dive into family matters and feel safe in its depths. This can be a highly secret part of your life.

Thursday 4th

Your emotions are too deep for you to process, so you just let them happen. The Moon is making difficult connections and you will feel this intensely. Let them flow and go. Cry them out if you need to. Seek nurturing from your closest family members to help you.

Friday 5th

It's possible that you feel the first effects of Mercury retrograde today. The Moon makes a poor connection to the messenger and any communication you have with a loved one will be misunderstood. Don't take anything too personally right now. Find the good from this situation.

Saturday 6th

Lady Venus sits with Saturn today. This has the effect of smoothing the edges of a tough situation. You have the patience and respect required to learn from an elder. It's a great time to discover how far your personal boundaries stretch and how far you can go with another.

Sunday 7th

Venus can't use her magic on someone in the workplace. An elder or person in authority can be unpredictable today. You're fighting off the urge to kick back and relax. There are jobs outstanding that need your attention before bedtime. You can't rest until these are completed.

Monday 8th

Mercury has nothing to say today as he is in the heat of the Sun. It's your job to listen to messages and observe dream symbols now. Your inner voice may be telling you things and you must discern the truth from your negative self-talk. Listen well.

. . . .

Tuesday 9th

The Moon meets Pluto giving your emotions a boost in transformations and endings. Is there something you now need to let go of? Pluto can help you do this. Good connections to Mars and Neptune mean that you have the drive and means to dissolve what's holding you back.

Wednesday 10th

The Moon enters your relationship sector and meets up with all the planets staying there. Your mood could be up one minute and down the next. This is unsettling but will last no more than the day so stick with it. Ride the tide of emotions that surface.

Thursday 11th

A New Moon in your relationship sector also connects to Mercury in retrograde. Be aware that intentions set now concerning this area are unlikely to stick. The better news is that Venus and Jupiter, the planets of love and luck, meet up and wish you well. This is big love.

Friday 12th

Your intimacy sector is touched by the Moon today. You may feel like reaching out to others or having an ethereal time floating around on your own. Be brave and go deeper and further than you have before, you might surprise yourself. Treat yourself to a delicious meal with good company.

Saturday 13th

A dreamy mood takes over your day. Neptune has caught you and whisked you away to a desert island. Mercury retrograde meets with Venus and any misunderstanding with a lover is quickly forgiven. You may share a dream and talk nonsense with them, it doesn't matter today.

Sunday 14th

The surreal mood continues until the evening for you. You're diving for pearls and finding them. Mercury meets Jupiter and the mental chatter or dream-like conversations you have been having expand. It will be hard for you to get grounded again before morning and the working week begins.

Monday 15th

You're fired up and outgoing today. The energy of the Moon in your travel sector has picked your mood up and you reach out to the wider world. Saturn and Jupiter make you responsible yet open to anything new. If you come across elders or authority figures, listen to them.

Tuesday 16th

Have you taken on more than you can deal with? Don't let that Leo pride prevent you from backing away from something now. A project can be shared with a loved one or business partner, taking some weight from you. Transform or end what is too heavy.

Wednesday 17th

As the Moon enters your career sector it meets volatile Uranus again. Your emotions can get the better of you. However, this is also the best time to come up with new and innovative ideas for work you are passionate about. Are you an emotional wreck or a genius today?

Thursday 18th

Your emotional state from yesterday will pick up pace now as the Moon meets Mars. You can be a force to be reckoned with in the workplace. It's possible that you are responsible for leading the pack and motivating others now. Don't let outside influences get in the way.

Friday 19th

The planetary energy is very unstable today. Venus and Mars are arguing and Saturn and Uranus are having a stand-off. All of this will affect your relationships and career. If your closest relationships are in business, prepare for a tumultuous ride. There will be bloodshed at some point.

Saturday 20th

You get some relief as you are able to offload to friends. Talking about your problems or simply letting off steam with your friendship groups can relieve tension. The Moon in your social sector is chatty and wants to connect on a superficial level. Bounce ideas around with friends.

Sunday 21st

Mercury finally turns direct. You have a chance to assess any collateral damage and try to make amends. As the Moon is making a nice connection to Venus, your first stop might be with your lover. A cosy night together will end the week nicely for you both.

Monday 22nd

In your hidden sector are all the secrets you keep to yourself. One of those is how you wish to be taken care of. You need to know that this sector is protected from harm and so you never reveal much about it. Self-care and nurturing are what you need now.

Tuesday 23rd

Warm, fluffy jumpers, fantasy TV shows, home cooking and bubble baths. If you can manage any one of those today, you will be happy. Even fierce lions need to wallow or nest at some point. This can be a dreamy day which fills you with feel-good endorphins.

Wednesday 24th

Today you stand up and say a firm no to something which goes beyond your comfort zone. Mars lends you self-assertion as you oppose Pluto who wants something from you. This is coming from your health and duties sector. Others may be demanding your service at great cost to your comfort.

Thursday 25th

Venus drifts into your intimacy sector like an ethereal mermaid. However, you are too busy to notice. You'll be forgiven for feeling paranoid and victimised today, the Moon in your own sign is making unhappy connections to all the planets opposite. Get up and roar or hide until it is over.

Friday 26th

Today brings lighter energy but you may still be feeling rattled. Use the Moon in your sign to be the star of your own show. Try to light up the room when you enter. Smile at people for no reason. Be brave and courageous.

Saturday 27th

A Full Moon in your sector of finance, value and possessions will highlight all the tiny details. You can be congratulated for keeping a tidy home, desk and bank account. This lunar month will show how you serve others willingly, sometimes too willingly. Any health problems will show up now.

Sunday 28th

Powerful earth energy is surrounding you and asking that you get more grounded today. Simply get out in nature, go for a walk, do some yoga or meditation. You will have the drive to do something practical now, despite Neptune's best efforts to seduce you into fantasy thinking.

MARCH

. . . .

Monday 1st

Navigating all that you need to do today comes easily. There are helpful connections from the Moon to the planets in your relationship sector. You're able to communicate shared visions with responsibility. This is a good day to plan future events as you are both on the same wavelength.

Tuesday 2nd

Your emotions are balanced and your mind is seeking expansion. Think about any intellectual avenues you would like to explore. You're recalling skills you learned in the past and what you would now like to learn. Many ideas fill your mind and excite your neurons. Reach out now.

Wednesday 3rd

Time spent at home or with family may be problematic. The Moon sits opposite Uranus and is at odds with Saturn. Expect the unexpected or tantrums will shock you. This can be resolved by using Venus' influence in your intimacy sector. Find your empathy and restore harmony.

Thursday 4th

Family life continues to be somewhat intense. There's just no satisfying some people here. Do no more than you need to, let other people pull their weight today. You may be seeing through another's eyes and understanding what triggers them. Unconscious material surfaces for you to deal with.

Friday 5th

Are you feeling creative today? The outgoing Moon in your expression sector opposes Mars. This is a great day to put any tension into art or words. Mercury and Jupiter meet and conversations with a lover or partner can touch subjects far and wide. This is an active day.

Saturday 6th

Self-expression comes in many forms today. This can be words of love or grand gestures. On the negative side, this influence can make you larger than life and boastful. The rebel in you may come out and demand action. You might need to find your soapbox now.

Sunday 7th

As the Moon shifts, you settle back into neglected duties. You may be whizzing through the day getting all the odd jobs done. Climbing a mountain begins with a first step. You'll accomplish great things today and may even surprise yourself. Good work deserves a reward. Treat yourself.

Monday 8th

Your work ethic is distracted by Neptune today. Are you dreaming of switching off and doing something just for yourself? Look at where you're sacrificing your own time. Try listening to your inner voice today and use it as a guide. An in-depth conversation with your soul is needed.

Tuesday 9th

Pluto says hello to the Moon today. This meeting can tug on your emotions and remind you of what needs to change or end. When the Moon shifts, your relationships may feel the brunt of this. Don't be hasty. Let this mood pass and review your thoughts.

Wednesday 10th

The Sun meets Neptune today. Under the heat, the mist of illusion that Neptune creates evaporates. You now see something important and intimate in a new light. As the Moon passes by Jupiter and Saturn, you are emotionally challenged to be optimistic yet stern. Be cruel to be kind today.

Thursday 11th

Your heart needs a chat with your head today. It may be difficult for you to relate to important people. Feelings need to be processed before you can connect to another in a meaningful way. This evening, the urge to connect is strong yet you are afraid to approach people.

Friday 12th

The Moon in your intimacy sector makes you deeply empathic now. You are searching your psyche for ways to connect to something bigger than yourself. It's possible that you seek spiritual enlightenment or at least a tribe of like-minded souls. Your unconscious is stirring you into this action.

Saturday 13th

A New Moon in your intimacy sector may be just what you were looking for. Use this opportunity to set intentions and goals. Neptune connects and asks that you surrender and learn to go with the flow of your emotions. Pluto is also on hand to empower you.

Sunday 14th

Venus meets Neptune now. This influence is dreamy and surreal. You will find yourself being swept away by enticing promises. Be careful that you don't drift too far. Don't be tempted to self-medicate, try meditation or yoga instead. A fiery Moon can help you keep your eye on the ball.

Monday 15th

Plans for new experiences are high on your list today. You have a mind to conquer new lands, absorb new religions and taste exotic cultures. This is far more grounding and natural to you than your recent thoughts. Get out your planner and start making notes.

Tuesday 16th

The Sun connects to Pluto making you feel good about changes you need to make. However, the Moon's poor connection to Pluto fills you with doubt. These conflicting messages need to be filtered. Remember that the Sun is your ruler and the Moon passes quickly. Your emotions will soon change.

Wednesday 17th

You ground yourself by focusing on your work today. Every task is completed meticulously. Slow and steady is the flavour of the day. Outside influences such as a boss or authority figure may rattle you but do not alter your productivity. Keep at it, this is good for you.

Thursday 18th

It's hard to be optimistic today. There's no joy coming from your relationship sector and you may feel unsupported in the workplace. Look to Venus and Neptune and remember that there are times when you have to trudge through the day and there are times for release and fantasy.

Friday 19th

Your social sector is visited by the Moon for the weekend. You may be extra touchy today and need to let off steam. Friendship groups, including online, can be good places to rant. Mercury and Mars can help you express yourself in an assertive way. Let out your anger safely.

Saturday 20th

Today is the Spring Equinox. This is a time to pause and reflect before the Sun shifts into fiery action. Consider everything now and hold that tension like a coiled spring. The Sun enters your travel sector and will energise any plans for travel or higher education whilst here.

Sunday 21st

Do you feel like a caged lion today? Venus has entered your travel sector and is now the warrior queen. She will add harmony, balance and maybe money to any plans you have for expanding your world view. However, it's not going to happen all at once.

Monday 22nd

The Moon drops into your hidden sector and gives you some relief. Buying something that makes you feel good or your favourite food enhances any alone time. Nurture yourself now or visit your mother or older female relatives. Intuition is strong and feminine wisdom is worth listening to today.

Tuesday 23rd

You have a need to self-protect or shy away from the crowds today. Neptune and Pluto make you conflicted. Is there someone from your relationship sector who is being passive-aggressive? You may need to switch off any contact and be alone with your thoughts now. Look after your personal boundaries.

Wednesday 24th

Planetary energy is unstable today. The Moon is in your own sign so you will feel this acutely. The well-wishing planets send you strength and empathy, but the volatile planets lurk ready to block your progress. Stick with it, this will soon pass and you will feel better.

Thursday 25th

Jupiter has something to say to you today. He sits in your relationship sector opposing the Moon. It's possible that your fierce inner lion has been made to look like a pussy cat by someone throwing their weight around. Be courageous and stand up for yourself now.

Friday 26th

Pull your attention inwards and do mundane things such as checking your bank balance, decluttering and food shopping. Mars in your social sector may get you going to the gym with friends. He asks that you think about a new exercise regime. Try it, you may enjoy it.

Saturday 27th

Are you being pulled in different directions now? This is your heart being indecisive. You must do what serves you best and not take anyone else into consideration. Pluto is helping you with self-control because you're at risk of running off to fantasy land thinking under Neptune and Mercury's influence.

Sunday 28th

Today there is a Full Moon in your communications sector. This will illuminate anything you have strived for in this area in the last six months. Where have you achieved balance? Have you acted as a mediator in a situation? Venus is opposite reminding you to act with love.

. . . .

Monday 29th

Authority figures may be singing your praises today. Your social life may get a boost of energy and big plans may be made. Party invitations are looking good and you may already be revved up to go. Whatever is brewing in your friendship circles, it's big, very big.

Tuesday 30th

A deep, intense Moon brings you back to family issues. Be careful, this shift also means that Uranus the disruptor is awakened. Hurtful interactions can be explosive. Mercury meets Neptune, watch out for deceivers and liars. If something seems too good to be true, it probably is.

Wednesday 31st

The Moon connects to Mercury and Neptune today and you find it hard to separate fantasy from reality. Have you been told some gossip or a secret? The detective-like Moon in your family sector will root out the truth at all costs. The Sun, your ruler gets help from teacher Saturn for this.

APRIL

. . . .

Thursday 1st

You get extra discipline from Saturn today and this helps to put you on the right track for a productive day. The Moon in a fellow fire sign has no time for emotions. You are expressive and self-serving now. Romantic overtures may come from your courageous heart today.

Friday 2nd

A mission awaits you. Mercury is having talks with Pluto, this will soon be revealed. Thoughts from the past come back and haunt you momentarily. Your social sector is having some bother from assertive Mars, but you are stepping away from it. Do the right thing today.

Saturday 3rd

The Moon and Mercury are at odds. This is because they both wish to connect. This influence can cause misunderstandings with a loved one. Don't take it too personally as this will pass quickly. Sidestep this issue by attending to a mountain of small tasks that await you.

Sunday 4th

Get grounded today because this evening you may get an idea of Mercury's mission for you. He's at the very last degree of the zodiac and, just as the Equinox needed you to pause and reflect, Mercury now needs you to listen. Make a note of your dreams tonight if you can.

Monday 5th

Control issues or power struggles may be possible today as the Moon meets Pluto. Consider this as your relationship sector is highlighted this afternoon. Mercury also connects to the Moon and lets you know that your new mission concerns your one to one personal or business relationships.

Tuesday 6th

Venus and Mars are playing nicely today. Your travel and social sectors are linked somehow. You may benefit from spending time with an elder you respect. They have wise words to share. Be careful not to rock the boat at work today. Disruptive Uranus is playing dangerous games with partnerships.

Wednesday 7th

Today is a great time for expanding your vision or getting to know someone better. Romantic partners give you food for thought. Is it possible that you may have met someone spiritual? You're a keen student and nothing will stop you from learning what you want to know.

Thursday 8th

You may have a crisis of conscience today. The Moon is squaring off with the points of fate, past and present. Karmic baggage may need to be released or reviewed. With Uranus' help, you can make this shift easily with few disturbances. Be at peace with your past now.

Friday 9th

Your energy is drawn two different ways today. On the one hand, you wish to spend it offloading or on physical activity with friends. On the other, you wish to hang around in Neptune's depths and do nothing. You will benefit most from some alone time.

Saturday 10th

Getting up and out is a big change from yesterday but you are motivated by your partner. Planetary connections between your relationships sector and your travel sector influence your choice of activity. Planning vacations or education courses seem to be on the agenda. This energises you. What will you plan?

Sunday 11th

The Moon meets Mercury today. Your mind is simply filled with ideas now. You must take some time to process these and consider which are achievable and which are not. Choose wisely. Thankfully, you have Saturn helping and making sure you make responsible choices.

Monday 12th

A New Moon in your travel sector gives you the confirmation you need to put your ideas into solid plans. Venus is on hand to give balance and harmony. Your drive is strong and you're highly excitable. Get rid of old projects that no longer thrill you and make space for these new ones.

Tuesday 13th

The Moon enters your career sector and you must pay attention to your responsibilities now. Remember that whatever new plans you have, this is where your security comes from and you can't jeopardise that. You may be unable to sit still today when the Moon meets unpredictable Uranus.

Wednesday 14th

Venus is at the last degree of your travel sector. She asks that you are sure that your new plans align with your true self. If this feels good and gives you great self-esteem then it is right for you. Your workload may get bigger today but so may the rewards.

Thursday 15th

Venus has now stepped into your career sector where she will be the lady boss. The good news is that while she is here, she can enhance your finances and get you seen as a valuable team player. You are already in weekend mode and chatting with many friends.

Friday 16th

Reviewing your social sector is a good activity to do today. Do you have the right friends around you? How can they help you advance? You're drawn to a possible future now and need to know that your social acquaintances will be there for you. If not, then it's time to change that.

Saturday 17th

Today's energy is very mixed. Dissatisfaction from within your social groups can make you hungry for change. You have a lot of mental processes going on right now. Mercury is busy connecting to planets in your relationships, career and duties sectors. Don't make decisions lightly.

Sunday 18th

The Moon now in your hidden sector where you can spend time alone with your thoughts. Strangely, all is quiet. Mercury is in the heat of the Sun and is simply listening. Be like Mercury, observe with your eyes and ears, you might be surprised at what you discover.

Monday 19th

The Sun and Mercury move into your career sector together. This heralds a month of being the best you can in the workplace. Let yourself be seen and heard if you wish to advance your career. There can be business trips and a lot of networking for you now.

Tuesday 20th

The Moon lands in your sign and you can be paranoid. It may feel like all eyes are on you, especially at work where Venus and Mercury are right now. If this is the case, be sure to perform well and meet all your deadlines. Impress those above you now.

Wednesday 21st

Your uneasy feelings continue today. Saturn the great teacher is opposing the Moon. The best thing you can do now is to listen well to any advice from an elder or person in authority. Leos make great leaders, so show what you're capable of. Start by being willing to listen.

Thursday 22nd

Mars is at the final degree of your social sector. Before he moves, it's critical that you use your energy wisely. Do your friends support and encourage you to be assertive or do they make you irritable? This can be a busy day of meetings and showcasing your talents.

Friday 23rd

Venus and Uranus meet up today. They have a board meeting at work. The Moon connects to both in a very helpful way. Planners come out, checklists are ticked and harmony is achieved. You are being assessed by superiors. Venus grants you the gift of self-worth.

Saturday 24th

Mars is in your hidden sector now. It's likely that you'll hold a grudge and not speak about it for a while. Thinking is foggy this morning but clarity resumes when Mercury meets Uranus and you get an 'aha' moment. Two heads can come up with something innovative today.

Sunday 25th

You may be on a high note today. Venus and Mercury want to make a date and enjoy some luxury. Maybe a celebration is in order. It's possible that you may spend too much as these two are connected with finances. Spoil yourself, but be sensible with your money.

Monday 26th

The Moon is in your family sector and deep feelings can come up to be healed now. Pluto is connected and you may see power struggles. However, Jupiter and Mars make helpful connections bringing you a lot of energy and optimism. There is joy to be had from your family today.

Tuesday 27th

A very intense Full Moon occurs today. It will oppose the planets in your career sector. You must review your relationship with money, love and how you place value on things. There is something crucial about this Moon. What needs to be transformed or discarded now?

Wednesday 28th

Pluto goes retrograde today in your health and duties sector.
Take this as a clue to what it is you need to change or bring an
end to. If you don't do it consciously, Pluto will do it for you.
Look at things from a different angle before taking action.

Thursday 29th

The Moon is in your creative sector. You're fired up right now
and eager to get out and do something. Create, write, paint
or impulsively tell someone that you love them. The Moon
joins the point of past karma and you know what it is that
needs to go.

Friday 30th

The Sun, your ruler, meets Uranus today. This is highly volatile
energy. At worst, you may experience tantrums or shocking
news. At best, this energy is fertile for breakthrough ideas
and new inventions. Rebellions may start now too as the Sun
represents your ego. Either way, this is a memorable day.

MAY
. . . .

Saturday 1st

Your emotions are guided by the Sun and Uranus meeting up. This is ongoing and is likely to dominate your weekend. If the drama is outside of you, the best thing to do would be to concern yourself with odd jobs and little things that have been neglected lately.

Sunday 2nd

Venus and Mercury are telling you to have some fun today. Be responsible but allow yourself to spend some of your hard-earned cash on a little treat. You may be an example to someone who does not manage their finances well. Fun does not have to be costly.

Monday 3rd

Trouble or tension in the workplace can affect your love life and vice-versa. It's possible that you come up against a wall and cannot move forward. If Uranus has any influence today, you can break through but must accept the consequences. An ego clash is very likely so be compassionate.

Tuesday 4th

Mercury is at the final degree of your career sector. You must ensure that all jobs are finished off and communication is clear before he moves. The Moon in your relationship sector makes you more emotionally invested in your lover but may also pull you away from your work duties today.

Wednesday 5th

Today you may experience your feelings increasing towards someone. The Moon meets Jupiter and expands your heart. You wish to extend your borders and take a relationship to the next level. The depth of emotion you feel now can disturb you. Getting intimate can help release some tension.

Thursday 6th

Your day may feel somewhat surreal today as you simply drift through on autopilot. You will need to stay on-task somehow. Jupiter is on the final degree of your relationship sector. This luck-bringing planet wants you to be sure of your feelings before he bounces into your intimacy sector.

Friday 7th

The weekend buzz starts early for you as you come out of your dream-like state and need action. Make plans for activities which are energetic. Venus helps you to keep loving what you are doing at work whilst Pluto helps to bring the week's tasks to an end. A busy weekend awaits.

Saturday 8th

Mercury is now flitting around in your social sector. This is a great time to network with new connections or simply catch up with existing friends. Mars is sulking in your hidden sector and wants to join the action. You may experience some jealousy or a boisterous newcomer who pushes boundaries.

Sunday 9th

Venus glides into your social sector. She has a harmonising influence on your friendship circles. Now is the time to share the love and invite new people to join you. Love may be found amongst your social groups. Prepare for a lot of engagements with both Mercury and Venus here.

Monday 10th

The Moon comes to your career sector to begin the week. This makes you steadfast and dependable. Uranus says hello and, as usual, can mean disruption or genius thinking. It's possible for you to break a code or solve a puzzle now. Well done.

Tuesday 11th

A New Moon in your career sector gives you the opportunity to set new career goals. These can be long or short term goals but you will need a game plan and sustained effort. This is not a quick fix. Aim for the stars but work hard for them.

Wednesday 12th

The Moon will also join your social sector for the next couple of days. Today there is a ladies meeting with Venus. Female friends and acquaintances can be highly productive or influential. Tension between your friendships and romantic relationships can arise and you'll need to prioritise your time with each.

Thursday 13th

Today you have an excellent opportunity to speak your mind. What is it you are passionate about that can raise fury in you? Mercury lends you eloquence so if you need to prepare or make a speech, now is the time. You can be quite the orator and impress people.

Friday 14th

Jupiter moves into your intimacy sector, expect deeper and wider interactions. You will find that you are inclined to go soul-searching with Jupiter here. The mysteries of life will seem more accessible to you. They pique your interest more than before. Keep an eye on your financial investments now too.

Saturday 15th

You have a relatively quiet day today. The Moon dips into your hidden sector and you may wish to spend time alone with your thoughts. Introspection will serve you well and with a helpful connection to Jupiter, you may already be diving for pearls from your psyche.

Sunday 16th

Intrusive thoughts can keep you awake today. The Moon meets Mars who has itchy feet and does not like to be kept in. Old beliefs and childhood conditioning come up for review. This isn't comfortable for you. Treat yourself to comfort foods to help you get through the day.

Monday 17th

The week begins with the Moon in your own sign. You can relax now and get back to routine and what is familiar. However, this takes a lot of self-control because the Moon is opposite Pluto who is asking you to deal with something deep. You can do this.

Tuesday 18th

A resistance to lessons from your elders causes you to feel blocked. This influence from Saturn can also mean that you or someone else has breached a personal boundary. Ask for guidance from your social groups, a wise friend will help you deal with this and offer a compassionate ear.

Wednesday 19th

You may want to take a closer look at how you present yourself today. Yet again, you come up against opposition from a person in authority. It's likely that something within you is being triggered and the problem is you and not the other.

Thursday 20th

A tidy home and bank balance give you the security you desire. It's worth spending some time today doing some personal admin. A thorough clean-out of anything you no longer need can give you the emotional stability you need right now. If it doesn't please you, let it go.

Friday 21st

The Sun, your royal ruler, is now in your social sector. Invitations sought by Mercury and Venus will fill your schedule. The Sun also deals with ego so be careful not to get involved in personality clashes over the next month. You have a busy mind today.

Saturday 22nd

There is time today to strive for balance. You may be asked for your valued opinion and will have to remain objective about an issue. Short journeys and messages may fill up the day and help to get a clear view of a dispute. Brothers and sisters need you now.

Sunday 23rd

Saturn, the teacher planet, goes retrograde today. This will mean that you need to review boundary issues in your relationships for the next few months. You come across someone from your social sector who is not what they seem. Don't get drawn into the illusion they have created.

Monday 24th

Your mood turns deeply inwards. The Moon is in your family sector and this can get too intense for you. Turning your attention to your work may not help today as the opposition to disruptive Uranus may niggle at you. Don't avoid issues with family that need your attention.

Tuesday 25th

Today you may see the first effect of Saturn retrograde. Your home life and personal relationships are at odds now. This is a test for you. Mars helps you to be firm and say what is on your mind. You may even tell reveal a secret of yours.

Wednesday 26th

A fiery Full Moon in your creative sector highlights your achievements over the last six months. How have you learned to express yourself honestly? You are being seen by those who matter, and you give a good impression. What you have been seeking, you may well have found today.

Thursday 27th

You're self-centred today and can be a little obnoxious. People from your social sector will point this out to you. Argue your case if you must but know that the energy is not favourable for you. You may be under an illusion of greatness and blowing your own trumpet.

Friday 28th

See to the nitty-gritty daily jobs today. Routine suits you and helps when you need to lie low and lick your wounds. Have a quiet day working through your task list. Check in with your health now and write a shopping list for healthy, immune-boosting foods.

Saturday 29th

The trickster Mercury goes retrograde today. He first visits Venus and together they discuss what needs to be reviewed in your social groups. Back up your devices and double-check travel plans. Be mindful that communication can go awry when Mercury turns, pause before responding to difficult people or say nothing.

Sunday 30th

A Sunday spent with a loved one may just the medicine you need today. The Moon makes lovely connections to the Sun and point of fate. Conversations can be filled with optimism and future plans together. Remember that Mercury has turned, ensure your words and thoughts are communicated clearly.

Monday 31st

In your relationship sector, the Moon meets retrograde Saturn. You may find that you're pushed out of your comfort zone. Perhaps it's you that is doing the pushing. Mars and Neptune connect making you or someone else force intimacy where it may not be wanted.

JUNE

. . . .

Tuesday 1st

Your royal ruler, the Sun, meets the point of fate today. It's possible that you get an idea of where you need to be heading in life. What excites you? What is your true calling? Emotions can run deep as Jupiter sits with the Moon and expands them

Wednesday 2nd

Venus enters your hidden sector today. Here she will nurture you like a heavenly mother. She will teach you how best to nurture yourself as an adult. Your self-love and self-worth will be enriched now. If you desire time alone, Venus will show you how best to fill it.

Thursday 3rd

Today can be difficult as you are pulled in various directions. A desire to merge with like-minded folk is rudely interrupted by tension from your social sector. Mercury is already causing trouble. You may need to pause and see things from a different perspective.

Friday 4th

You have more energy and are revved up ready for the weekend. You can ignore anything too good to be true in your social sector and concentrate on the huge joy you are feeling from going within and doing your inner work. Success elevates your spirits and you shine outwardly.

Saturday 5th

Mars and Pluto combine to knock you out of your happy place today. You may have a conflict between your own inner processes and how you interact with someone special. A choice must be made which may mean that you compromise your own values. You don't have to make sacrifices.

Sunday 6th

The two luck bringing planets, Venus and Jupiter are making great connections to the Moon today. Your sense of responsibility and ability to earn money or provide is enhanced. Enjoy this moment and use it to your advantage. Buy yourself a treat, maybe some ice-cream.

Monday 7th

You may feel up against deadlines and under stress at work today. Uranus is making you bubble under the surface however this could also be a great new idea you have been germinating. Saturn feels like a harsh boss but notices all the good work and sustained effort you give.

Tuesday 8th

Do you feel as if you're being left behind? Worry not, you aren't the only one. The energy today is full of change, assertiveness and impermanence. Go with the flow and see where you end up. This could be an interesting day for networking with new ideas.

Wednesday 9th

Your social groups come up with a source of intrigue for you today. This could be something simple such as planning a social event. It could also be something deeper where your interest groups are following a new thread of learning. Join in and let it feed your imagination.

Thursday 10th

A New Moon in your social sector collides with Mercury retrograde. This starting point combined with the trickster asks that you pay a great deal of attention to who you keep company with right now. Listen to those who inspire you and dump those who drain you.

Friday 11th

Mercury is in the heat of the Sun now. He has nothing to say but your mind may be full of chatter. Filter messages you get and file some away to deal with later. Mars marches into your sign and will make the next few weeks invigorating or exhausting.

Saturday 12th

The Moon meets Venus in your hidden sector. How well have you looked after yourself recently? If it's possible, have a pyjama day and spend time alone. Switch off with your favourite TV show or book. One day off will not hurt you, it will do you good.

Sunday 13th

People will try and pull you out of your nest today. That lion's roar may not be far away when you need it. Defend your right to self-care and time alone. Stand up for yourself and you may well be surprised at how this adds to your self-worth.

Monday 14th

Social groups may be teetering on the edge of fantasy thinking. There could be someone amongst them who is bewitching and beguiling you. You need not be led astray if you remember to stand your ground and not self-sacrifice. The fog will lift soon, and all will become clear.

Tuesday 15th

Another day of strength and courage for you. You are handling this Mercury retrograde well. Saturn and Uranus are squaring off so prepare for some upset between work and an important partner. It may be that your energy has had enough of certain people and you now choose to say so.

Wednesday 16th

You may have a mini-crisis today when you think of how hard it was for you to dismiss people from your life. This is all part of cleaning up the clutter that surrounds you. You begin to look at what Venus has taught you about self-worth and see how it all fits.

Thursday 17th

Serving others of your own free will is highly regarded. Offering yourself up for sacrifice is not. The Moon sits opposite Neptune who can teach us this difference. This is something that crosses your mind today. Try stilling your mind and changing your perspective on this issue.

Friday 18th

This morning you feel much more balanced emotionally. Use today to get all the small jobs done. This may mean you make a lot of short trips but you are in control and Mars in your sign gives you the energy to steamroller your way through the day.

Saturday 19th

Do not lose sight of Venus' lesson today. The Moon connects to Mercury and Saturn, both retrograde in sectors concerning relationships. This is another test that you should take notice of. You may be triggered and old childhood habits return to protect yourself. These are no longer useful to you.

Sunday 20th

Jupiter now goes retrograde. This huge planet ruling expansion, truth and optimism will challenge what it means to connect to others in a meaningful way. The Moon is in your family sector and is at odds with Mars. Are too many people demanding your time and energy again?

Monday 21st

The Summer Solstice marks the longest day of the year. The Sun enters your darkest hidden sector. Expect old wounds to be re-opened this month but use this energy to soothe them. The Sun will highlight what you are ready to bring up from your psyche and heal.

Tuesday 22nd

Mercury ends his retrograde cycle and tension lifts from within your social groups. Your creative side is illuminated and your passions nag at you. What do you love doing and have neglected lately? Try to find your soul urges and re-connect with the inspiration that drives them.

Wednesday 23rd

You are driven to get out the paints or explore a new location today. The poet inside you is aroused. Your head and heart have a chat and as Mercury is direct, your thought process is more clear. You may have trouble saying no to people today.

Thursday 24th

A bright Full Moon in your relationship sector shows what you has come to fruition in the last six months. What started small and is now a mountain. What is bigger than you could have imagined? Do you now need to make a cull and strip away anything unnecessary?

Friday 25th

Today Neptune goes retrograde. This will make your intimacy sector fuzzy and unclear for a while. If you bear this and you can refrain from making bad choices, Neptune will offer you many delights now but not all are real. Check finances you share with another as there could be something amiss.

Saturday 26th

Power and control become issues again today. Venus is asking that you sit tight and do not compromise yourself. An intruder wishes to take advantage of your pussycat side. Remember that you are a lion too and do not be afraid to let others see that side.

Sunday 27th

Today it's difficult for you to keep your anger under control. Mars in your sign is opposite the Moon and Saturn. You may be feeling caged and need an outlet. Uranus chips in to add to your volatile mood. Venus enters your sign and tries to pacify you.

Monday 28th

Relationship matters may have come to a head recently and you are still angry or upset. Check in with your emotions now as they may be bigger than they need be. Find a just cause to put that energy into. Try to re-connect with people or spiritual practice.

Tuesday 29th

You have a lot of thinking to do today but you cannot seem to gain clarity on anything. Do not try too hard as this will tax your brain even more. Confusion can cause you to get angry again. Be still and empty your mind until this passes.

Wednesday 30th

Today you are being asked to listen to your inner voice. The Moon and Mercury are squaring off making it tricky to listen to your heart and your head. Neptune invites you to listen within. This isn't one of his temptations, this is a skill he wishes to teach you.

JULY

. . . .

Thursday 1st

Mars in your sign just wants action but today is opposing
Saturn who firmly puts him in his place. This will make you
very frustrated. You have a list of things you need to get on
with and all you see are blockages. Mars' energy can make
you volatile.

Friday 2nd

More favourable aspects help you to get the last-minute jobs
done. You become a powerhouse of activity. Speaking to people
in your wider groups helps you to offload any tension in a safe
place. Do you need a holiday? A yearning for new places to
explore fills your heart.

Saturday 3rd

This afternoon you may be spending money on luxury items.
Don't invest funds with another today, go solo if you must.
As you are self-conscious about spending, your luxury item
could be work-related or the latest bit of technology. Relax,
spoil yourself with something you want but don't need.

Sunday 4th

Today the Moon squares off with Venus and Mars, both in
your sign. You may have needs which come across as selfish
to others. Uranus says hello to the Moon and brings about
something unexpected. It's likely that you go over the top with
your spending today.

Monday 5th

In your career sector, the Moon makes connections to Neptune and Pluto. There is a possibility that what once looked like a good thing is now causing you some regret. Did you keep the receipt? The Sun, your ego, supports your needs but your rational self does not.

Tuesday 6th

Today you're networking or socialising more than usual. Are you the one responsible for making future plans for your friendship groups? Your thinking is not clear now as you may not have all the facts. Retrograde Jupiter asks that you ask others to help you find you more information.

Wednesday 7th

Venus now opposes Saturn. You will find it difficult to remain balanced and composed today. Relationships are not in sync at the moment. Saturn is sitting there asking you to re-evaluate how you behave with people who are important to you. Try not to act out today.

Thursday 8th

Filtering information you hear today will reap benefits at a later date. Not everything you hear is true. Neptune wishes to whisk you away to fantasy land, but you need to keep a clear head. This afternoon the Moon dips into your hidden sector and you desire to be alone.

Friday 9th

Today you must nurture and protect yourself. You may be very close to erupting into tears or taking your frustrations out on someone at work. Perhaps you have had enough of adulting and want to be looked after. Shop for your favourite foods and enjoy an evening at home.

Saturday 10th

A New Moon in your hidden sector gives you the chance to review how you've been spending your private time. Something needs to change now as this Moon is opposite Pluto who likes endings or transformations. Set intentions to make improvements concerning your self-care and personal boundaries.

Sunday 11th

The Moon comes into your sign and you can be self-centred or the life and soul of the party. You wish to express yourself unfiltered and let off some steam. However, there is opposition from your personal relationships. Check in with yourself, this may be your shadow acting out and not another person.

Monday 12th

If you go with the flow, today can be great for romance. Venus and Mars are both touched by the Moon and you are emotionally invested in connecting with another. Reaching out to a loved one can result in a mutually beneficial evening. Your energy and emotions are in sync.

Tuesday 13th

This is another harmonious day for love. Venus and Mars meet up in your sign. What you desire and what you want come together effortlessly. The Moon shifts to your money and values sector. This energy combined with the celestial lovers' means that you are made to feel precious today.

Wednesday 14th

The love vibe continues. You question how partners can serve each other equally. If you are happy for a relationship to be in the form of a contract, then this may be the freedom you desire. You and a partner need to know the score in order to thrive.

Thursday 15th

The Moon and Sun both make connections to Neptune today. As Neptune sits in your intimacy sector, this energy can make you feel truly merged with another. At the moment it is dreamlike and surreal but remember that Neptune can cast illusions and dissolve your sensibility. Stay grounded today.

Friday 16th

Communications may be thwarted today as the Moon squares off with Mercury. Your hidden sector is now hosting Mercury who loves to explore here. If you have something deep and meaningful to say, it may come across wrong and you may be misunderstood. This is a brief phase.

Saturday 17th

A harmonising Moon in your communications sector whispers romantic words to you. Make the most of this energy as it helps ensure that everyone is thinking clearly. This evening is different however, Pluto connects to both Sun and Moon, you may see an ego clash, or something forever transformed.

Sunday 18th

A deeply intense Moon in your family sector means that you may want to withhold information from your nearest relatives. You are bursting to speak out but think better of it. This energy within you is sizzling, try getting out and doing something active to disperse it wisely.

Monday 19th

Today you are feeling extra dreamy, on cloud nine even. Remember that Neptune is trying to make you see what is real and what isn't. If in doubt, do something earthy and grounded such as walking in nature. This evening your fiery, passionate side may be expressed with childlike laughter.

Tuesday 20th

Even though your mood is outgoing and expressive, you take a moment to look back at skills you have learned in the past. You may now wish to revive a project which was once important to you. Mercury and Uranus are connecting, watch what you say, or you may regret it.

Wednesday 21st

The Moon makes another great connection to Venus and Mars.
Your current artistic temperament could see you writing love
poetry. Venus is at the end of her stay in your own sign, use
her energy to ensure that your emotional wellbeing is balanced
before she moves on.

Thursday 22nd

The Sun enters your sign today, this is your birthday month,
happy birthday! Venus enters your finance and values sector
and will help you to love what you have or get rid of anything
which no longer serves you. Prepare for a thorough clear out
while she's here.

Friday 23rd

Have you been neglecting your health? This is a good time to
get a check-up or renew your subscription to the gym. The
Moon meets Pluto and they discuss what bad habits you've
acquired without realising it. What can you change about your
daily routines and lifestyle?

Saturday 24th

A Full Moon in your relationship sector throws a spotlight
on important one-to-one connections. It also shows you your
shadow aspects and how you project onto others. Something
may come to a head or be complete now. The Moon also meets
Saturn who will ask you to review this.

Sunday 25th

Today you may feel rebellious and want to do your own thing. Uranus, Mars and Pluto are shaking things up and asking for change. Mercury has unearthed something from deep within your psyche and is asking you to justify it or heal it. Mars and Uranus want action now.

Monday 26th

In your intimacy sector, the Moon meets retrograde Jupiter. Deep feelings may seem larger than you are able to deal with. They sit opposite Venus so you may feel undervalued today. This influence can also mean that you have a heavy workload due to taking on chores for others now.

Tuesday 27th

Pause, take time out and breathe. Neptune is visited by the Moon and is asking you to listen to your inner voice. Ask Neptune to dissolve anything that is disturbing your thought processes. It's likely that you've become attached to something which is not helping you.

Wednesday 28th

Mercury jumps into your sign today. You will be extra chatty now. Your mind, if cleared from debris, will become a hive of ideas waiting to be manifested. Mercury's stay in your hidden sector brought up some issues of how you need to protect yourself, now you are putting it into practice.

Thursday 29th

Jupiter has retrograded back into your relationship sector.
You must now review where the joy is missing, or the
optimism has gone. What can you do to bring them back?
Mars sits opposite and is eager for action. Make sure that
assertiveness does not turn into aggression.

Friday 30th

Mars is now in your money and values sector. If you are not
getting what you think you deserve, Mars will help you step up
and ask for it. A fiery outgoing Moon in your travel sector is
busy with inquiries. What new thing can you learn now?

Saturday 31st

Your career gives you security and today you may have some
concerns about that. The Moon sits there today and makes
uncomfortable connections. This phase will soon pass so don't
waste time worrying. Get all the facts and make a plan B if it
helps. You may be worrying over nothing.

AUGUST

······················

Sunday 1st

Today it's important that you listen to your courageous heart. Stress may be thrown at you from the workplace and you may feel you're about to blow. Mercury is in the heat of the Sun and asks that you listen. An elder has something to teach you too.

Monday 2nd

The weekend's gone but you're already reaching out to the next. Are you burning the midnight oil trying to meet deadlines? The Sun in your sign opposes Saturn now, this energy can feel like a strict teacher or boss expecting great things from you.

Tuesday 3rd

Emotional support comes from your wider groups today. These can be friends you go out with or online groups with similar interests. You get some ideas on how to go forward with your life and live out your true purpose. Your self-worth can be low today, give yourself a treat.

Wednesday 4th

Mercury in your sign is asking you to get things off your chest. This concerns your work and social status. Don't be dragged into unrealistic thinking now. Make your point clearly and without apology. Try not to be selfish or brash as this will not do you any favours.

Thursday 5th

A quieter day today leaves time for some introspection. You bravely take a good look at your triggers and corresponding behaviours. Mars can help you work through this methodically and declutter your mind. Remember to look after your own needs today, ice cream and a good TV show can help.

Friday 6th

The monthly opposition between the Moon and Pluto makes you feel powerless. This is not true; Pluto is simply asking that you transform an unhealthy way of thinking into a more positive one. Venus is ready to help in your sector of self-worth. Keep your ego out of this.

Saturday 7th

The Moon slips quietly into your sign and you feel more stable. However, a Leo Sun is squaring off with Uranus in your career sector. This could mean that you have found your lion's voice and are ready to let it roar. You may have an 'aha!' moment now.

Sunday 8th

Today there's a New Moon in your sign. This is a fantastic opportunity for you to set life goals and intentions. There's no stopping you today as you break down barriers and aim for the stars. You should create a vision board to be proud of.

Monday 9th

The Moon meets Mercury who already knows what it is you want. An opposition to Jupiter means that you can over-think or over-inflate your plans. Come back down to earth for a moment and re-think your vision. Make it realistic and attainable to avoid disappointment at a later date.

Tuesday 10th

The Moon meets Mars and your enthusiasm remains high.
This may be a day where you declutter ruthlessly. Venus and
Neptune are in opposition; Neptune's trying to make you keep
hold of absolutely everything whereas Venus knows what will
serve you best. Forget what ifs and let stuff go.

Wednesday 11th

The Moon and Venus are having lunch in your finance and
values sector. You take a very hard look at what's around you
and how you value it. If your money situation is concerning
you, ask Venus to help you increase it. Perhaps you can sell
stuff you have decluttered.

Thursday 12th

You are feeling much more at peace now. Although there may be
many errands to run or people to see today, you know you have a
harmonious home to come back to. Mercury has landed in your
finance and values sector. Business ideas will come to you now.

Friday 13th

It is possible that you have to be firm with someone who may
be trying to manipulate you. Although you are happy to run
around for others, sometimes you can't see when you are
being taken advantage of. Bring this to an end with a firm
message today.

Saturday 14th

You are closed off today and not giving anything away.
Boundaries may be pushed but you are strong enough to
push back and stay intact. Mars lends you his strength and
assertiveness to stand up for yourself. Stay home alone and
avoid people who push your buttons.

Sunday 15th

Family life can get a little too intense for you. Tantrums and
tears are too close to the surface. You may feel like a small child
being reprimanded and wonder what you have done to deserve
it. Lie low until this energy passes and you feel grown up again.

Monday 16th

Venus now enters your communications sector. This is her
sign and she'll rule it like a boss. Your mind and emotions
are at odds today but rest assured that when the Moon shifts,
you'll feel more settled. Mercury has you looking back at the
past and towards the future simultaneously.

Tuesday 17th

You have a head full of ideas and a heart full of expression.
What are you going to do with them? Neptune is playing
games with you and casting a mist over your motivation. You
are raring to get on with something creative but lack direction
at the moment.

Wednesday 18th

The Moon in your creative sector is activated by Venus. She
asks that you forget your emotions and think logically. You
must do what is necessary today or nothing else will get done.
Duties, mundane jobs and health check-ups must be your
priorities over anything else.

Thursday 19th

Whilst the Moon is steadily making you climb mountains and
get things done, Uranus is turning retrograde. This can mean
that despite your best efforts to stay on track, something comes
along and derails you. Mercury and Mars have met, watch that
your mouth does not run away with you.

Friday 20th

You may now have some ingenious ideas to raise capital or beautify your home. Change is in the air. The Sun and Jupiter face off, watch out for ego clashes within your important relationships. It's likely that you have to be cruel to be kind today. Set standards for better relating.

Saturday 21st

The Moon in your relationship sector is squaring off with newly retrograde Uranus. Expect clashes between your career and your important relationships. As it's the weekend, is it really necessary to bring work home with you? You may be close to solving something and not want to put it down.

Sunday 22nd

Today there's an altruistic Full Moon in your relationship sector. This is at the final degree which means it's critical that you bring something to completion now. Did you want to join a rebellion but missed the boat? Build a boat for your own revolution.

Monday 23rd

Your emotions are all over the place today. The Moon in your intimacy sector wishes to merge with like-minded souls but your energy is drained. This can be a tearful day where you look back at what you've lost and forget to look at what you have gained.

Tuesday 24th

This is a day to pause and reflect. Your mind and heart are not in sync so the best thing you can do is to pause. There's a problem you need to solve, perhaps you need a fresh pair of eyes to see the solution. Wait for inspiration.

Wednesday 25th

You have more get up and go today. An outgoing Moon in your travel sector sees a way forward and is anxious to start. You desire to push on and see the wider world or at the very least, a wider picture of where you are right now.

Thursday 26th

If you feel a tugging from your relationships sector, tug back. Let them know who is in control of you. Jupiter asks that you broaden your vision and see where you are being slightly manipulated. The truth will out when you begin to make enquiries, start investigating now.

Friday 27th

You have an urge to treat yourself but feel guilty about spending money. If you're sensible, then you can do this without breaking the bank. An intimate dinner with a loved one or something to impress the boss will also please you. You deserve a little something.

Saturday 28th

Tell yourself that you're worth it today. The planetary energy asks that you continue to be kind to yourself with some luxury. Do something spontaneous and surprise yourself. Mars and Venus both help to give you the energy and motivation to do something nice for a change. Have an evening out.

Sunday 29th

Today you find that your imagination is filling you with fantastic ideas. Your social group can be a font of wisdom for you to draw on. They inspire you to find your true north and make the necessary changes in order to follow your own path. Get a checklist ready.

Monday 30th

The Moon meets the point of destiny and now you have some idea of what yours may be. Mercury enters your communications sector where he will be taking over the administration and making all the bookings for you. Your calendar is about to become very full.

Tuesday 31st

You may be emotionally drained today. Your active mind needs to have some downtime. Time spent with friends in a light-hearted way will help take some pressure off. This is also an opportunity to put the feelers out and gain experience from others who may have done similar things to you.

SEPTEMBER

· · · · · · · · · · · · · · · · · ·

Wednesday 1st

Your instincts are to curl up in a warm, fluffy ball and ignore the outside world. However, there's not much rest for you today. Everyone needs your attention and there are jobs to be done. If you persevere, you are likely to be exhausted by the end of the day.

Thursday 2nd

Self-care must take second place today. You are in demand and must deal with this. Neptune is opposite Mars and is draining any energy you have left. The safety of your home beckons but there is so much to do. Work first and take a long, deserved rest later.

Friday 3rd

Your energy picks up just as the weekend approaches. People from your important relationships may pull you away from your seclusion but this may be exactly what you need. The Moon makes a nice aspect to Neptune in your intimacy sector. Drift off with someone special tonight.

Saturday 4th

The Moon is in your sign and lifts your spirits. The need to be quiet has gone and you are in party mode. Mercury helps you to connect with the right people today. An opposition to Saturn means that you rebel and do as you please. You may even shock yourself.

Sunday 5th

Let yourself be seen and heard today. Venus makes you feel good without being obnoxious or overpowering. Someone may try to bring you down, but you have the strength to realise this and stop it before it gets out of hand. You may need to establish boundaries with an elder.

Monday 6th

It's tidy-up time for you today. Getting all your affairs in order, decluttering your home and preparing a great shopping list is on the agenda. This is how you feel in control of your life. A tidy home environment is essential for you to function properly.

Tuesday 7th

A New Moon in your money and value sector is just the energy you need for an early Autumn clear out. The Moon meets Mars and you march on through your day with great confidence. Emotional satisfaction allows you to ignore the call of Neptune and fantasy thinking today.

Wednesday 8th

Balancing all your duties is easy now. You can cut through the fog and gain clarity with your no-nonsense approach to errands and short trips. People admire you for your responsible attitude and may even come to you for problem-solving advice. Personal relationships are on an equal footing today.

Thursday 9th

The Moon meets Mercury in your communications sector. You wear your heart on your sleeve and don't hold anything back. There's something that has been niggling at you and now is the time to speak. Jupiter links to the Moon and asks you to seek the truth of a situation.

Friday 10th

Venus gets a visit from the Moon today. They discuss how well
you have been taking care of yourself and recognising your
own worth. Self-judgement is not the goal here, self-praise is.
Do not under-sell yourself. Venus and the Moon glide into your
family sector together. This is powerful.

Saturday 11th

The intensity of the Moon and Venus is seductive now. This
may shake up a few out-dated family habits. Female Leos will
rule their pride fiercely. This is nurturing at its best with a
warrior-like defence mechanism all around you. Stand up and
roar, show them who you are.

Sunday 12th

Agitation from your personal relationships must be dealt
with fairly. There are lessons to be learned from saying no or
asking that people wait until you are ready to respond. You're
outgoing and eager to please but there are limits to what you
are willing to do for others.

Monday 13th

Honest conversation makes your job easy today. You have no
time for small talk or empty promises and would rather get
straight to the facts. Self-expression is the way to lead today,
as others will follow your example.

Tuesday 14th

Your royal ruler is opposite Neptune and burning away the mists of illusion. It's likely that you can see through a falsehood or spot a fake person easily. A person or event in your intimacy sector may now be exposed and this can be quite upsetting for you.

Wednesday 15th

Check in with your body today and ensure that you're getting enough rest, exercise and healthy foods. Don't make excuses. You may be tempted to ignore any health niggles and get on with your duties. This is avoidance and will not do you any good in the long run. Accept that you need to attend to this.

Thursday 16th

Issues of control may surface today. People will demand your time and take you away from your daily duties. Mars makes a good connection to the Moon enabling you to be assertive when you need to be. Late afternoon you are more inclined to spend time with someone special.

Friday 17th

This is a difficult day for love or business partnerships. Women will want their own way and can be tricky to deal with. Saturn meets the Moon and reminds you to be firm and adult with people who try to manipulate or pull you out of your comfort zone.

Saturday 18th

Go with the flow today. It's too easy to throw your hands up and rebel against the general mood of the day. Jupiter sits with the Moon making any emotional state you are already in much larger. Sit back and observe what it is that's pushing your buttons.

Sunday 19th

Today you wish to get to the very bottom of a situation. You could also be getting philosophical or simply inquisitive about life's mysteries. You may be seduced into spiritual thinking and possibly come up with bold, new ideas. You explore new intellectual territory today.

Monday 20th

A Full Moon will highlight issues in your intimacy sector. It connects to Neptune and you look at where you've been a scapegoat for others. Consider sacrifice and surrender and what they mean to you. You desire to merge with something bigger and more elusive. Imagination feeds you today.

Tuesday 21st

A fiery Moon fits your temperament better today. You are unused to ethereal thinking and prefer making plans and being active. Your desire for something outside of you takes you to land instead of spirit now. Travel plans or interest in other cultures grabs your attention.

Wednesday 22nd

The Autumn Equinox occurs today, and this is a time to pause and reflect. Mercury is squaring off with Pluto and this makes you think about any imbalance in your general duties to others. Are you communicating efficiently? Do people still take advantage of you? What can you change?

Thursday 23rd

The Sun is now in your communications sector. This shift only highlights what you have been thinking about. As a generous soul, this can cause you some grief as you do not like upsetting people. Tantrums from within your family sector are likely and you may be asked to mediate.

Friday 24th

You're emotionally drained today. Is it you who is having the tantrum? The Moon, your emotions, is sitting with Uranus and a volcano is getting ready to blow. Sit tight, this is a brief phase and you just need to ride the storm.

Saturday 25th

To make yourself feel better, you splash out on something nice. Get all your weekend chores done and let yourself relax. The Moon connects to Neptune who agrees that you need time off. Perhaps a tasty meal or a scented bath will do the trick. Watching a fantasy film will also help.

Sunday 26th

Mercury goes retrograde today. The usual advice applies; back up devices and double-check all travel plans. Think before you speak and clear up misunderstandings. Get out tonight and socialise. You have a little energy left for the remainder of the weekend. Interactions with friends can be lively.

Monday 27th

You may be chatty and indecisive at work today. Neptune is making your thought processes unclear and your conversations seem to go around in circles. This is nothing to do with Mercury, but he may be standing back and seeing how you deal with this. Think before you speak.

Tuesday 28th

Today you may see the first effects of Mercury retrograde as the Moon connects. Your wider groups, including online, may be busy with interactions. It may be hard to follow one thread. If a misunderstanding occurs, take a step back and pause before responding. Others may not be so thoughtful.

Wednesday 29th

The Moon enters your hidden sector. Your privacy is valuable to you now and you need to conserve energy. A connection between Venus and Neptune means that you feel romantic, seductive and wish to spend quality time with a lover. Surprise someone with an open invitation to your home.

Thursday 30th

The energy today is so watery and emotional that you may drift off to another dimension. If you're alone, then this is great for fantasy novels or films as you will immerse yourself fully in the thrill. If you have someone to share this time with, enjoy compassion and empathy.

OCTOBER

. . . .

Friday 1st

You're more empowered today as the Moon is back in your sign. An urge to push through boundaries and restrictions is irresistible and commendable if you need to be productive. However, leave personal boundaries untouched for now. Expect delays with communications and chores today as Mercury makes unhelpful connections.

Saturday 2nd

Be very careful in your dealings with people higher than you today. The Moon is opposing Jupiter who stands for law and order but also connects to Uranus the disruptor. Your leadership qualities may be challenged. If you're a weekend worker, be mindful of upsetting the boss.

Sunday 3rd

It's possible to make amends with someone today. Mercury is connecting to Jupiter. Remember that retrogrades are not meant to trip you up but are chances for you to 'do over'. Review, revisit and rethink a recent confrontation and put things right today.

Monday 4th

Money is on your mind now. Check any financial arrangements you have with another person as there may be a payment overdue. This is a good time to make sure your home affairs are in order even if it's just clearing a messy spot. You may discover something you thought lost.

Tuesday 5th

You make changes that affect your duties and obligations to others. This will free up some time for you to concentrate on your own interests. Well done, you're practising self-care by making time for yourself. These small steps will gain momentum until you're completely in charge of your schedule.

Wednesday 6th

Planetary energy is high today. There is a New Moon in your communication sector right next to Mars. Think of this as a supercharged time to make goals and intentions which will likely stick. Pluto turns direct and self-control will become easier. Mars and Pluto are formidable allies.

Thursday 7th

Venus is about to leave your family sector. Is there anything outstanding that needs attention here before she moves? Honour your female relatives and take note of any women's wisdom passed down to you today. A deeply nurturing and secretive Moon will take her place for the next two days.

Friday 8th

The Sun and Mars meet today and activity ramps up. Your communication sector will be busier than ever, but you have the energy from Mars to deal with it. There may be high productivity or massive ego clashes. Make sure that there are no misunderstandings and enjoy this energetic time.

Saturday 9th

This is a difficult day emotionally. First, you're tempted to switch off and do nothing, then you're reluctantly coaxed outside to join in some fun. Your creative and passionate side just wants to play today. Romance is favoured but be careful that playfulness doesn't turn nasty.

Sunday 10th

Saturn turns direct in your relationship sector today. This will ease some of the pressure and allow you to begin making moves to get to know someone better. The Moon connects nicely to other planets making this a day where you are more emotionally balanced. Have a peaceful day.

Monday 11th

Your energy is buoyant today and you start the working week with a smile. Projects that bring out your artistic side are easily tackled. People will admire the way you take on tasks and make them a priority. This is a happy day make the most of the energy.

Tuesday 12th

Expect to be pleasantly surprised at work. This could be that you discover something or solve a problem. You will be recognised as a dependable member of the team today as you work through the day steadily. Take small steps to begin a task which looks insurmountable.

Wednesday 13th

The Moon meets newly direct Pluto today. Issues of power and control come under discussion. Where might you have let someone else lead the way? Do you now need to take charge? They meet in your health and duties sector so this could also concern your personal wellbeing.

Thursday 14th

In your relationship sector, the Moon now meets Saturn, also newly direct. Partnerships will benefit from a frank discussion today. Over the summer months, relationships may have been strained but will begin to settle into a pattern which is mutually beneficial. This may feel unusual but will work.

Friday 15th

The Sun and Jupiter combine to bring you some good luck and advice today. Listen to any words coming from fathers, male elders or bosses as this will stand you in good stead in the long run. This stern paternal energy is also filled with joy and optimism.

Saturday 16th

The Moon enters your intimacy sector today. You contemplate where you're going from here. Do you wish to get to know someone or something on a deeper level or are you afraid to? The mysteries of life such as sex, death and rebirth both fascinate and repel you.

Sunday 17th

Jupiter turns direct today. You may experience this as a huge sigh of relief. If you've been confused about relationship issues weighing on you, you may now see a way forward. The Moon sits with Neptune making your emotions a little foggy but this will pass soon. Listen to your inner voice.

Monday 18th

The trickster Mercury turns direct now. While he has been in your communications sector, you may have had to slow down or pause your mental faculties. You have found this frustrating. Now you can think, plan and communicate without misunderstanding once more. An action-packed Moon will help.

Tuesday 19th

You're emotionally invested in doing something more valuable with your spare time. Long distance travel or higher education call you. The Moon sits opposite Mercury and you must now evaluate the long-term investments of study and travel. Perhaps you can combine these with a work vacation?

Wednesday 20th

There's a Full Moon in your travel sector today. This is the culmination of the last six months of planning and discovering. Has it been worthwhile? You may feel emotionally drained and despondent today. Maybe not all your goals have come to fruition. Don't beat yourself up about it.

Thursday 21st

You are feeling down, and tears may be very near the surface. Your work environment is not satisfying you today. The Moon sits with Uranus making you unstable, but you can also use this energy to come up with something new and innovative. Get up and make a difference.

Friday 22nd

Let yourself dream a little now. Replace negative thinking with something to cheer you up. Splash out on a fine dining experience and don't feel guilty about it. Use your hard-earned cash on something to make you smile. You may have to be coaxed to do this.

Saturday 23rd

The Sun enters your family sector and will warm up interactions here. In this deeply intense sign, you may find that people bond more or reveal their secret worries. Your social sector is visited by the Moon and you're desperate to connect with your wider groups and let off some steam.

Sunday 24th

Mercury and Venus are connecting to the Moon today. Your social life is full of plans and conversation. A lover may wish to do something different to the group and this could cause you some conflict. You will need Mercury's skills as a mediator to work around this problem.

Monday 25th

Your mind is very busy today. Active Mars is busy trying to keep everyone happy whilst optimistic Jupiter is attempting to appease problems with your relationship. Neptune tries to drag you away for some peace, but you are determined to make peace with others before getting time for yourself.

Tuesday 26th

Venus and Neptune are squaring off today. You may be acting out and having mini-tantrums with a lover. The Moon is in your hidden sector and you simply need to be left alone to take care of yourself. This may be more like licking your wounds, growl safely in your own home.

Wednesday 27th

When you are in self-protect mode, there is always someone who wants to pull you out of it. Practise what you've learned this year and come out when you're ready. Communications are too emotionally charged today, say nothing or risk a new cause to fight.

Thursday 28th

The Moon reaches your sign by late morning. Until then you may be extra sensitive and defensive. There's a risk that you show off and become obnoxious as your mood has not abated yet. Rules and regulations annoy you and your inner rebel rises. Sit tight, this will ease.

Friday 29th

Conflict in the workplace keeps you on your toes. You may find yourself arguing your case in order to keep the peace. Mercury is still in your communications sector and you can draw on his energy to help you speak honestly and clearly. Don't get drawn into unnecessary dramas.

Saturday 30th

Ego clashes are possible as the Sun and Saturn are at odds. Family members and important relationships need your attention. Mars has just marched into your family sector so expect the bigger pull to come from there. You feel stuck between a rock and a hard place.

Sunday 31st

You feel the need to bring order out of chaos. Built-up tension from recent days needs an outlet. DIY projects or a deep clean of your home will be worthwhile activities today. You know you always feel better by making a change or having a clear out of unwanted items.

NOVEMBER

. . . .

Monday 1st

Use your powers of persuasion to ask for what you want today. Mercury is making a helpful connection to Jupiter in your relationships sector. Think of a dream or vision you wish to share with someone special and vocalise it. You may just want to make a few small changes.

Tuesday 2nd

The Moon now dips into your communications sector and you are emotionally invested in sharing information which will help bring balance. What are you passionate about which needs to be heard by others? Stay in control but refrain from being pushy, elders are listening.

Wednesday 3rd

Mercury now greets the Moon. You may find that your heart and head are in sync and whatever comes out of your mouth does so with utmost conviction. You want fairness and equality now. It seems like it's up to you to address any imbalance that has transpired recently.

Thursday 4th

Today can be highly volatile or powerful. The New Moon in your family sector is asking for a big change, starting from now. Connections to Uranus and Mars mean that things could get disruptive. Use this powerful energy to brainstorm the best solution for all involved. No secrets, no lies.

Friday 5th

The Sun sits opposite Uranus and challenges the disruptive planet. You may witness a stand-off where someone has to account for their rebellious actions. Mercury is going to eke out family ghosts whilst Venus prefers that you simply do your daily duties and not get involved. This is a testing time.

Saturday 6th

Today you may feel creative or poetic. Your inner child wishes to come out to play. Take a break from adulting and enjoy some childlike fun. Venus reminds Mercury that if he must go opening old wounds, to do it with kindness and with a view to getting them healed.

Sunday 7th

Joyous Jupiter tunes into your need for play today. As the luck-bringer, he can see that you need to feel free, even if just for a little while. Don't let Neptune seduce you into switching off with things such as alcohol, keep it safe and enjoy some laughter today.

Monday 8th

The Moon and Venus have a ladies' night. Many planets connect to allow you to tap into feminine wisdom or enjoy the company of women. You have a list of small chores but can work through them steadily and be pleased with your results by the end of the day.

Tuesday 9th

You may now get an idea of what the New Moon brought up. What needs to change? Pluto is asking that you end something and clear the decks to make way for something new. If you're afraid of change and resist it, then Pluto will do it for you.

Wednesday 10th

This is a tricky day with tough planetary energy. You desire to reach out and feel the love with a partner but Mercury and Mars have met up. This energy can be very argumentative or sexually persuasive. Saturn is also involved, be very mindful of pushing people's boundaries.

Thursday 11th

The air is still sizzling with tension in your relationships. Uranus is waiting to blow it all up in your face. Jupiter jumps on board and can either make outbursts larger or disperse it all with his joyful nature. How you play it is up to you.

Friday 12th

The Sun in your intense family sector is burning away illusions set up by Neptune. It's likely that you will now see a situation for what it really is. Those ghosts in the family closet may be ready to be exposed. You feel stunned and do not know how to act.

Saturday 13th

Compassion and empathy are your two best allies today. There is still unsavoury stuff emerging from your family sector. You are asked to look at things from another's point of view. Mercury opposite Uranus does not help. This is unstable energy so expect rows and plenty of tears.

Sunday 14th

You're not comfortable with this emotional energy and need to be in your own element. This afternoon the Moon moves into your travel sector and offers you a distraction. Make plans for yourself, be selfish if it means disassociating with other people's dramas. Let your brain do the talking.

Monday 15th

Be aware that those close to you are watching how you handle conflict. You must be the leader that your fiery sign represents. It may be hard for you to get on with your daily routine, but you must do so for your own sanity. Stick to your agenda today.

Tuesday 16th

Resistance will come from your duties sector and interfere with the plans you are making in your head. You must double-check that you can commit to new ideas to travel or study. Perhaps this is not achievable, and you already have too much going on.

Wednesday 17th

The focus is on your career today and there too, you find blocks preventing you from realising your dreams. Mars is now opposite Uranus meaning that your roles at work and at home are under fire. Be sure of your responsibilities before taking off on your own path.

Thursday 18th

You are ready to blow today. Don't let temporary setbacks cause you to lose face and show your lion's roar. You may say something that you don't mean or shouldn't voice out loud. If you use this energy wisely, you may finally get to the bottom of something deep.

Friday 19th

A Full Moon in your career sector will put you in the spotlight. You are being observed so you must be on top form. Tie up loose ends and complete projects before the weekend arrives. Lighten your load and let those who are watching see how capable you are.

Saturday 20th

The Moon is in your social sector just in time for you to have some downtime with friends. If you stay home alone, your mind will be doing overtime and you won't switch off. Mercury and Jupiter connect making family interactions great fun or highly controversial, probably the latter.

Sunday 21st

During your interactions with your wider social groups, you may find that not all your dreams are possible. You might feel disappointed and need time to process this. Neptune is coaxing you to follow a path which is just an illusion. Get more grounded and get advice from friends.

Monday 22nd

You return to self-protect mode today as the Moon enters your hidden sector. Factor in some time to shop for your favourite foods and schedule a good book or film. The Sun has shifted into your creative sector. You may feel extra sensitive and need to express your deepest feelings.

Tuesday 23rd

Today you reflect on the years gone by and what you have left behind. This does not come without some sorrow. Venus wants you to get on with your daily routine and get some stability but you are wallowing in the past. Remember the good lessons you can use now.

Wednesday 24th

That familiar nagging takes you away from your comfort zone before you are ready. The Moon dips into your sign and you become resentful and sulky. Mercury leaves your family sector having dug up some dirt and leaving a big hole. Deal with it and heal it.

Thursday 25th

If you are open to it, today can be romantic and passionate. The fiery Moon in your sign opposes Saturn but you wish to connect with someone special. Venus and Mars make this possible by finding time to play nicely. Your ruler, the Sun, is in your romantic sector so take advantage.

Friday 26th

Be mindful of how you're putting yourself across today. You are bold and brash but may come across as selfish and narcissistic. Wanting your own way is one thing but do not do it at the expense of someone important to you. They will remind you of this.

Saturday 27th

Over the weekend, make yourself feel better by organising your home and finances. You're not in the mood for social interactions so use this time to declutter and check your bank balance. Decluttering your environment helps to declutter your mind. This will leave you feeling fresh and receptive.

Sunday 28th

Neptune nags at you to relax and kick back. Ignoring this call and continuing to do personal admin will serve you better. By the end of the day, you will be so pleased with yourself that you make an impulse buy and treat yourself. A simple takeaway meal will suffice.

Monday 29th

Mercury is in the heat of the Sun today. He talks to your
ruler and you have a good think about your recent behaviour.
Today's a day for listening and not speaking. Being quiet but
taking in messages from within you will provide you with
plenty of food for thought.

Tuesday 30th

Your emotions are more balanced today. There is some
resistance about doing your daily chores or helping someone,
but you don't take this too seriously. You have a duty of care to
others and you willingly oblige. You have time to relax and be
alone later today.

DECEMBER

· · · · · · · · · · · · · · · · ·

Wednesday 1st

Neptune moves direct today. A new Neptune cycle asks you to turn within and listen to your inner voice. Anything you have been struggling with in your intimacy sector will now become clearer. The deeper mysteries of life and your desire for something bigger will now be more tangible.

Thursday 2nd

Whilst in your family sector, the Moon connects to Neptune and you may see things with different eyes. This can be a revelation or an upset but will soon be smoothed over and peace will be restored. You may hear "I told you so" from an elder or a life teacher.

Friday 3rd

A meeting with Mars can make your emotions more volatile today. It can also provide fuel for brave, new action you need to take. You must be firm in your dealings with family. This afternoon it is easier to speak your truth with compassion and maybe even laughter.

Saturday 4th

Today there's a New Moon in your creative sector. An outgoing mood will help you set intentions to be who you truly are. Maybe you have an idea about what your sacred purpose is now. Listen to Mercury's messages as when he meets the Moon he may have some good advice.

Sunday 5th

A Sunday afternoon spent with a loved one can be pleasant.
You find that you're more willing to share your innermost
feelings. Discussions about where you would like to travel to
or what you desire to learn can be filled with joy and optimism.
Your partner shares your vision.

Monday 6th

One step at a time is the best way to achieve your goals today.
Tasks at work or in your daily life are near to completion.
Mars and Pluto connect to give you the strength and energy to
finish a long-standing project before the festive season begins.

Tuesday 7th

You may be emotionally invested in something that you now
need to let go of. Remember that when there is space, new
things can take shape. Pluto helps you to lovingly remove what
has reached its expiry date. You will have more time for love
and connection with special people.

Wednesday 8th

Today may be a little edgy when the Moon meets Saturn.
Think of a harsh teacher with a very important lesson for
you. You may not want to hear it but it's truly beneficial that
you do. Family, career and partnerships are all involved in this.
Be humble and listen.

Thursday 9th

Worries and concerns may feel bigger than they actually are.
A boss or leader might touch a sensitive spot in you today.
Take some time to pause and reflect on how you were triggered.
Self-talk doesn't need to be negative, praise yourself for the
good you have done.

Friday 10th

A more peaceful day today where you spend time contemplating
the last year. Revelations come but are gentle and make you
smile. There may be a nice surprise coming from your career
sector or a breakthrough of ongoing problems. Try not to fill
up your day with tasks.

Saturday 11th

Your mood continues to be dreamy and contemplative.
Spending time alone with your thoughts helps you to justify a
few things. Venus and Pluto meet up in your health and duties
sector. This is a day to put yourself first and pay attention to
your body. Listen to what it needs.

Sunday 12th

As the Moon shifts into your travel sector, you are more active
and begin making lists. A vision board of places of interest can
be a fun activity. The Venus and Pluto connection asks that you
make changes with solid steps to reach your goals. Don't let
anyone sway you.

Monday 13th

Two planets change sign today. Mercury now enters your health and duties sector helping you research any missing information you need. Mars marches into your creative sector and can either bring you the energy to stand up for yourself or can make you amorous and look for love.

Tuesday 14th

A small setback halts your plans today. You have a moment of conscience and wonder whether you are being too selfish. Your sense of security depends on your career income and you don't wish to jeopardise this. Wait until you have all the facts that Mercury will bring.

Wednesday 15th

Tension is building inside you. This is your old way of thinking and you must remember that it no longer serves your best interests. Take time to breathe and get grounded today. Take a walk in nature, do yoga or spoil yourself with an impulse buy just for you.

Thursday 16th

You put your worries to one side as there is too much going on now that the festive season approaches. Self-control helps you to work through your task list with ease and time spare to dream. If dreaming about a possible future makes you happy, keep doing it.

Friday 17th

The Moon dips into your social sector just in time for some weekend fun. You're in demand now and there will be a lot to chat about with friends you may not have seen for a long time. An opposition to Mars can mean that your social interactions will drain your energy.

Saturday 18th

Venus turns retrograde tonight. She will do this in your health and duties sector. You may find that you forget how to look after yourself now and burn the midnight oil. Expect a lover from the past to suddenly make a reappearance. Squabbles with a lover are possible now.

Sunday 19th

A Full Moon in your social sector will highlight the culmination of a project with friends. Maybe a course of study has come to an end. This can be a lively time with your online interactions and wider groups. By this evening you want your own space.

Monday 20th

The Moon in your hidden sector connects to Mercury and Uranus today. It's possible that something you would prefer to be kept secret is revealed and upsets you. Alternatively, you may wish to disclose something about yourself and this courageous action surprises you. Stay safe and keep your boundaries strong today.

Tuesday 21st

The Winter Solstice is here. The longest night is a time to lie low and contemplate. Treat yourself to home comforts as much as you can today and celebrate the longer days to come. Do whatever it takes to feel protected even if that means avoiding certain company.

Wednesday 22nd

Your sign is visited by the Moon for the final time this year. You feel more outgoing and join in the celebrations of the season. You can shine like a true leader today. Be warned, your tendency to go over the top can make you obnoxious. Lead with compassion and a true heart.

Thursday 23rd

Jupiter is at the final degree of your relationship sector for the second time this year. It's critical that you answer his call to sort something out once and for all. Remember that Jupiter stands for truth, justice and expansion. If you wish to know someone better, tell them.

Friday 24th

Tension is building as you would expect at this time of year. The areas affected for you are your home and finances. Do not be forced to host the celebrations if you cannot afford to. Be firm with people and tell them exactly how much you are prepared to do.

Saturday 25th

Venus returns to meet Pluto today. This is synonymous with control issues concerning women. Is there someone who is doing more than their fair share? Is this you? Ask for help or step in and give assistance to another. Make the day go without unnecessary hitches.

Sunday 26th

You just cannot rest today. You are like a prowling lion in a cage. If you're in your own home, you clear up any mess caused by the celebrations. You don't like to let it linger. This afternoon brings you back to a balanced frame of mind.

Monday 27th

The Moon in your communications sector helps you to deal with short trips and messages. Maybe the social side of the celebrations isn't over and you still have people to see. You have the energy to do your duty by your family and you behave like a responsible adult. Well done.

Tuesday 28th

The energy is much more difficult today. You do your best to make sure that all around you are happy but you cannot please everyone. Power struggles come from your health and duties sector and spoil the day. Let others sort their own problems out now.

Wednesday 29th

The Moon is in your family sector and your mood may be intense. Saturn and Uranus are involved so expect to be involved in a disturbance. Jupiter bounces into your intimacy sector where he'll make you inquisitive about life's deeper mysteries. Get ready to explore the depth and breadth of everything.

Thursday 30th

It's possible that you can use persuasive words to control a situation which may have got out of hand. Mercury is with Pluto and between them, they investigate what may have gone wrong. You will be completely drained by evening. Get some rest.

Friday 31st

Mars gives you the energy you need to party through the night. You can let off steam and thoroughly enjoy the evening. As the Moon has met Mars today, a New Year romance could be out there waiting for you. Have a great New Year's Eve.

Leo

. . . .

PEOPLE WHO SHARE
YOUR SIGN

PEOPLE WHO SHARE YOUR SIGN

. . . .

Leonians have studded the stage, ruled the roost and brought laughter and fun into people's lives for decades. Whether they choose to be actors or are royalty (or, in the case of Meghan Markle, both), Leonians shine in the spotlight. Discover the courageous and sparkling stars who share your exact birthday, and see if you can spot the similarities.

23rd July

Daniel Radcliffe (1989), Paul Wesley (1982), Kathryn Hahn (1973), Monica Lewinsky (1973), Marlon Wayans (1972), Philip Seymour Hoffman (1967), Slash (1965), Woody Harrelson (1961), Jo Brand (1957)

24th July

Turia Pitt (1987), Mara Wilson (1987), Elisabeth Moss (1982), Anna Paquin (1982), Rose Byrne (1979), Danny Dyer (1977), Jennifer Lopez (1969), Kristin Chenoweth (1968), Amelia Earhart (1897), Alexandre Dumas (1802)

25th July

Paulinho (1988), James Lafferty (1985), Shantel VanSanten (1985), D.B. Woodside (1969), Matt LeBlanc (1967), Iman (1955), Estelle Getty (1923), Rosalind Franklin (1920)

26th July

Stormzy (1993), Taylor Momsen (1993), Kate Beckinsale (1973), Jason Statham (1967), Sandra Bullock (1964), Helen Mirren (1945), Mick Jagger (1943), Stanley Kubrick (1928), Aldous Huxley (1894), Carl Jung (1875), George Bernard Shaw (1856)

27th July

Winnie Harlow (1994), Taylor Schilling (1984), Jonathan Rhys Meyers (1977), Tom Kerridge (1973), Maya Rudolph (1972), Nikolaj Coster-Waldau (1970), Triple H (1969), Julian McMahon (1968)

28th July

Harry Kane (1993), Cher Lloyd (1993), Soulja Boy (1990), John David Washington (1984), Alexis Tsipras, Greek Prime Minister (1974), Lori Loughlin (1964), Hugo Chávez, Venezuelan President (1954), Jacqueline Kennedy Onassis (1929)

29th July

Joey Essex (1990), Fernando Alonso (1981), Josh Radnor (1974), Wil Wheaton (1972), Sanjay Dutt (1959), Tim Gunn (1953), Geddy Lee (1953)

30th July

Joey King (1999), Yvonne Strahovski (1982), Jaime Pressly (1977), Hilary Swank (1974), Christine Taylor (1971), Christopher Nolan (1970), Simon Baker (1969), Terry Crews (1968), Lisa Kudrow (1963), Laurence Fishburne (1961), Arnold Schwarzenegger (1947), Henry Ford (1863)

31st July

Victoria Azarenka (1989), B. J. Novak (1979), Emilia Fox (1974), Antonio Conte (1969), J. K. Rowling (1965), Wesley Snipes (1962), Louis de Funès (1914)

1st August

Jack O'Connell (1990), Bastian Schweinsteiger (1984), Jason Momoa (1979), Ryoko Yonekura (1975), Coolio (1963), Yves Saint Laurent (1936), King Abdullah of Saudi Arabia (1924), Herman Melville (1819)

2nd August

Charli XCX (1992), Edward Furlong (1977), Sam Worthington (1976), Kevin Smith (1970), Mary-Louise Parker (1964), Wes Craven (1939), Peter O'Toole (1932), James Baldwin (1924)

3rd August

Karlie Kloss (1992), Charlotte Casiraghi (1986), Evangeline Lilly (1979), Tom Brady (1977), James Hetfield (1963), Martha Stewart (1941), Martin Sheen (1940), Terry Wogan (1938), Tony Bennett (1926)

4th August

Cole and Dylan Sprouse (1992), Crystal Bowersox (1985), Meghan, Duchess of Sussex (1981), Anna Sui (1964), Barack Obama, U.S. President (1961), Billy Bob Thornton (1955), Louis Armstrong (1901), Queen Elizabeth the Queen Mother (1900)

5th August

Olivia Holt (1997), Jesse Williams (1981), James Gunn (1966), Mark Strong (1963), Pete Burns (1959), Maureen McCormick (1956), Neil Armstrong (1930), Joseph Merrick (1862)

6th August

Charlotte McKinney (1993), Ferne McCann (1990), Robin van Persie (1983), Vera Farmiga (1973), Geri Halliwell (1972), Michelle Yeoh (1962), Barbara Windsor (1937), Andy Warhol (1928), Lucille Ball (1911), Alexander Fleming (1881)

7th August

Helen Flanagan (1990), Rick Genest (1985), Abbie Cornish (1982), Charlize Theron (1975), Michael Shannon (1974), David Duchovny (1960), Bruce Dickinson (1958), Wayne Knight (1955)

8th August

Shawn Mendes (1998), Princess Beatrice of York (1988), Roger Federer (1981), Meagan Good (1981), Chris Eubank (1966), The Edge (1961), Dustin Hoffman (1937), Emiliano Zapata (1879)

9th August

Bill Skarsgård (1990), Anna Kendrick (1985), Audrey Tautou (1976), Gillian Anderson (1968), Eric Bana (1968), Whitney Houston (1963), Michael Kors (1959), Melanie Griffith (1957), Jean Piaget (1896)

10th August

Kylie Jenner (1997), Brenton Thwaites (1989), Devon Aoki (1982), JoAnna García (1979), Angie Harmon (1972), Justin Theroux (1971), Suzanne Collins (1962), Antonio Banderas (1960), Juan Manuel Santos, Colombian President (1951), Herbert Hoover, U.S. President (1874)

11th August

Alyson Stoner (1993), Jacqueline Fernandez (1985), Chris
Hemsworth (1983), Anna Gunn (1968), Joe Rogan (1967),
Viola Davis (1965), Hulk Hogan (1953), Steve Wozniak (1950)

12th August

Cara Delevingne (1992), Mario Balotelli (1990), Tyson Fury
(1988), François Hollande, French President (1954), George
Soros (1930), Cantinflas (1911), Erwin Schrödinger (1887)

13th August

DeMarcus Cousins (1990), MØ (1988), Sebastian Stan (1982),
Alan Shearer (1970), Debi Mazar (1964), John Slattery (1962),
Prime Minister of Cuba Fidel Castro (1926), Alfred Hitchcock
(1899), Annie Oakley (1860)

14th August

Brianna Hildebrand (1996), Nick Grimshaw (1984), Mila
Kunis (1983), Paddy McGuinness (1973), Halle Berry (1966),
Emmanuelle Béart (1963), Magic Johnson (1959), Steve Martin
(1945), Doc Holliday (1851)

15th August

Jennifer Lawrence (1990), Joe Jonas (1989), Ben Affleck
(1972), Anthony Anderson (1970), Debra Messing (1968),
Melinda Gates (1964), Alejandro González Iñárritu (1963),
Anne, Princess Royal (1950)

16th August

Evanna Lynch (1991), Cam Gigandet (1982), Frankie Boyle (1972), Steve Carell (1962), Madonna (1958), Angela Bassett (1958), James Cameron (1954), Charles Bukowski (1920)

17th August

Taissa Farmiga (1994), Austin Butler (1991), Thierry Henry (1977), Donnie Wahlberg (1969), Helen McCrory (1968), Sean Penn (1960), Robert De Niro (1943), Mae West (1893)

18th August

Maia Mitchell (1993), Frances Bean Cobain (1992), G-Dragon (1988), Andy Samberg (1978), Edward Norton (1969), Christian Slater (1969), Patrick Swayze (1952), Robert Redford (1936)

19th August

Ethan Cutkosky (1999), Christina Perri (1986), Melissa Fumero (1982), Fat Joe (1970), Matthew Perry (1969), John Stamos (1963), Gerald McRaney (1947), Bill Clinton, U.S. President (1946), Gene Roddenberry (1921), Coco Chanel (1883)

20th August

Demi Lovato (1992), Andrew Garfield (1983), Ben Barnes (1981), Amy Adams (1974), Misha Collins (1974), David Walliams (1971), Fred Durst (1970), David O. Russell (1958), Joan Allen (1956), Robert Plant (1948)

21st August

Bo Burnham (1990), Hayden Panettiere (1989), Robert Lewandowski (1988), Usain Bolt (1986), Laura Haddock (1985), Carrie-Anne Moss (1967), Kim Cattrall (1956), Kenny Rogers (1938), Wilt Chamberlain (1936)

22nd August

James Corden (1978), Rodrigo Santoro (1975), Kristen Wiig (1973), Richard Armitage (1971), Adewale Akinnuoye-Agbaje (1967), Ty Burrell (1967), Honor Blackman (1925), Ray Bradbury (1920)

23rd August

Jeremy Lin (1988), Kobe Bryant (1978), Julian Casablancas (1978), Scott Caan (1976), Ray Park (1974), River Phoenix (1970), Rick Springfield (1949), Gene Kelly (1912)